Summer Days with Daughter

Books by Eugene Platt

Poetry
coffee and solace (1970)
Six of One/Half Dozen of the Other (with John Tomikel, 1971)
Allegheny Reveries (1972)
an original sin (1974)
South Carolina State Line (1980)
Summer Days with Daughter (1999)

Anthologies
A Patrick Kavanagh Anthology (1973)
Don't Ask Me Why I Write These Things (1974)
The Turnings of Autumn (1976)
Metamorphosis (1977)

Fiction
Bubba, Missy & Me (1992)

Summer Days with Daughter

New and Selected Poems: 1968-1999

Eugene Platt

Hawkes Publishing

Charleston, South Carolina

Acknowledgements

For previous publication of some of the poems in this book, grateful acknowledgement is made to the following: *The Above Ground Review, The American, Arizona Highways, Ball State University Forum, Bitterroot, The Blackbird Circle, Capella* (Ireland), *The Cardinal Poetry Quarterly, Caryatid, The Charleston Gateway, Charleston Magazine, Christianity and the Arts, The Club, Crazyhorse, Creativiti, Encore Magazine, The English Record, Flamingo, The Francis Marion Review, Gryphon, Icarus* (Ireland), *Insight, Jubilate Deo, Kudzu, Liaison* (Ireland), *Monument, Now, Oil City Derrick, Old Hickory Review, Omnibus, Outer Banks Current, The Paper, Pocket Poetry, Poem, Poet* (India), *Poet Lore,* The Poetry Society of South Carolina, *Point, Preservation Progress, The Review, Saint Andrews Review, Sand Castles, Sandlapper, The Shore Review, The South Carolina Magazine, The South Carolina Review, The Southwestern Review, Stone Drum, Sword of Light, Tar River Poetry, TCD Miscellany* (Ireland), *Tinderbox, Voices International, Wind,* and *Woodwind.*

I thank Bob Ivey and the Robert Ivey Ballet for choreography and public performance of some of these poems. I thank the Virginia Center for the Creative Arts for a very productive residency. A number of these poems were begun or revised at VCCA. My heartfelt thanks also go to Mepkin Abbey, a Trappist monastery, for a week-long retreat that strengthened my spirit as well as some of these poems. For various kinds of assistance, I thank Vanessa Cramer, Susan Davis, Trudy Evans, Carol Furtwangler, Jim Hawkes, Constance Pultz, Mark Wallace, Jed Waterbury, Dr. Mary Luton, and The Citadel Writing Center.

Library of Congress Catalog Card Number: 99-96577
ISBN: 0-918091-42-X (paper) / 0-918091-41-1 (cloth)
First Edition
Printed by: McNaughton & Gunn, Inc., Saline, Michigan
Book design: All About Graphics, Mt. Pleasant, South Carolina
Typeface: 11 pt. Bookman on acid-free paper

Foreword

the seasons slip away
faster
than I can flip my calendar

—which is to say the years of my life are passing quickly. Indeed, almost twenty have passed since publication of *South Carolina State Line*, long since out of print. Turning sixty last February brought home to me the prudence of publishing another collection while there is still time . . . .

And, in case there's not another opportunity, I pay special tribute now to all the children and young people who have had such an important role in my development as a writer. In week-long poets-in-the-schools residencies in five states, as well as in shorter visits to dozens of schools at all levels, I interacted with thousands of these highly creative human beings. In the process, many of my own poems germinated and I was blessed with the belief that what I was doing was worthwhile.

Prominent among those to whom I pay tribute are my own daughter Troye and son Paul, who have inspired some of my best poems and given me immeasurable encouragement. Troye is the kind of person who picks up and adopts stray unicorns. She was four that foggy morning she looked out the window and asked, "Daddy, did a cloud fall down last night?" A couple of years later, she came up with the most reasonable, as well as most poetic, explanation I have ever heard for the theory of the expanding universe when she made this out-of-the-blue observation: "The sky never ends because God's still making it."

Paul, meanwhile, was not mute. At age two, during a period when hot air balloons were seen frequently flying over our neighborhood, he teased me with the beautiful metaphor I have tried to convey in the poem "Metaphors Be With You." As our family watched television one evening a year later, he gleefully pointed at a Mississippi River steamboat on the screen and exclaimed, "Hey, look at that boat with the merry-go-round on the back!"

If poets ruled the world, we would decree such endearing memories of summer days with daughter or son for everyone.

Eugene Platt
October 1999

Contents

for Mary

Saturday Night Fare

Class B Westerns
at the Majestic Theatre:
a weekend ritual of cowboys
and Indians,
cattle rustlers routed by Red Rider,
or grand Tom Mix outwitting Mexican bandits.

Afterwards,
the King Street newstand,
a child's wonder library of comic books.
With my allowance
I always bought two—and ice cream
with the remaining nickle, while Dad sipped a beer.
(He was not only a fun pal,
but also my financier.)

If I live a thousand years,
I shall never forget
the legacy of love that was
our Saturday night fare

Melontime

Backyard vampires
freed for summer vacation,
we flew from schools,
our mouths salivating
and sharp teeth bared,
to attack fleshy bodies
filled with tasty red;
then, having fed
on seedy marrows,
quickly left the ruined
rinds as relished mementos
of a Southern season

Listen

Before learning geography
or names of any other railroads,
I knew the Atlantic Coast Line
like a song played late
in the Lowcountry nights of boyhood,
long low notes of locomotives
pulling trainloads of wanderlust
nocturnally along narrow tracks
        across the broad expanses
  of snaky swamp   marsh   woodland
      west and south of Charleston,
their mournful horns heard
by other boys too, from Maine
    to the tropical tip of Florida,
psyche-satisfying sounds that came through
the damp dark air lying stagnant in summer,
echoing now along a deserted track
           between my years

My Father

My father the musician,
singing "You Are My Sunshine"
and making melodies
on a Sears & Roebuck guitar.

My father the machinist,
as conscientious at the Navy Yard
as at home, putting his best
into a perfectly meshing gear.

My father the good neighbor,
sad and somber after nearly
getting stricken Mr. Crabtree
to the emergency room in time.

My father the lover,
often too tired to say it,
working his ass off
to show he cared.

Folly Beach Hotdogs

Folly Beach hotdogs
—probably the world's best
except, maybe, those you relished
in your own hometown's playground.

I often wonder
what made them so great.
I guess it was the onions and mustard
—and the sand, a grinding reminder
to ten-year-old gourmets
that with every bite
we were devouring
Folly Beach hotdogs.

Summers later
my interest turned
from hotdogs to cool girls,
the ones who safely stationed themselves
sixty feet from the surf,
hiding behind sunglasses and feigned disinterest.

I loved them seasonally,
but a fellow can only have shallow love with shallow girls,
and I was looking for something deep——
                              like
                                  the
                                      sea.
                    Folly girls weren't for me.

Youth's gone now—
the youth that surfboarded in this morning
was washed out to sea with the noon tide
of imminent middle age.

I still come to the beach,
but I walk farther,
down past the hotdogs and cool girls.
I walk until I come to a lonely spot
to share only with a couple of sea gulls
                    and a crab or two.
There I spread an olive drab blanket
and break open my soul
                    to sun itself
                              in the softer sunshine
                              of late afternoon

Main Crops, South Carolina

A weed is number one now,
and our Baptists grow the best tobacco
in this may-be-harmful-to-your-health union.
In the past we've cultivated rice,
indigo, and tradition.
Cotton has lost its crown,
but still is treated with runner-up respect.
A lot of us raise cabbage,
two hundred-proof corn,
and, on occasion, a little Cain.
We plant 'taters, 'maters, and, when necessary,
our neighbors.
Our melons make the modest blush,
and even Eve would be tempted
by the fruits from our farms.
O man, this state is great for peaches
and all the pride you can eat.

Edisto Hours

Fighting back against time,
the creeping thief
of your affection
for each other,

you deserted its citadel
for a space of timelessness
in the anachronistic marsh
of Edisto Island,
a place where clocks are valued
only as curios
and television sets are worth
less than a memory.

That brief eternity
let you look beyond yourselves
and there you found
the moments you sought . . .
                    just in time

Quartet for an Unholy Southern City

I

Three centuries of darkness,
lighted now in tricentennial
celebration, but even so,
you still cannot see that these three
hundred years have proved only
the viability of your bigotry.

You have crucified life on a
calvary of intolerance,
and life has left you to flounder,
adrift in your own cherished sea
           of non-conformity.

II

No status seeker, you covet
only the quo, content to drown
in a dream of your past—
no, not to sink, but to lie still as time's
tide engulfs without distinction.

III

For a quarter of a century
I walked your cobbled streets,
a loyal but blind son,
pointing out to visitors the charm
of ancient churches flanked by ragged
flower vendors and asking, "Where else
do you see such women selling flowers on streets?"
until answered one day,
"Where else do they have to?"

IV

Then I had the audacity
to advance the view—not new,
but too bold for the old town—
that perhaps dermal pigmentation
was not a valid criterion
upon which to judge a person's worth
or even the legitimacy of his birth.

Opponents of this heresy
wrote to me of their disapproval
one night—anonymously, of course.
They wrote symbolically with spray
of red paint on the side of my white Thunderbird.
I heard their hammer and sickle message.

Preservation Society

The painting invites your contemplation:

Symmetry. Serenity. Slavery.

Art does not happen in a vacuum—
so, consider the source of its inspiration:

Symmetry. Serenity. Slavery.

If not tempered by compassion,
life in a society committed to preservation
of its past can be conducive to askew
perspectives and incongruities go unnoticed:

Symmetry. Serenity. Slavery.

Facing a finely wrought sketch
of these symbols of Southern heritage,
you feel a surge of admiration
for an English immigrant artist
who made a string of slave quarters
a thing of ante-bellum beauty:

Symmetry. Serenity. Slavery.

Later, locked into your privacy,
you allow a mirrored image of yourself
to look you in the eye and shame you
into a reconsideration of that response:

Symmetry. Serenity. Slavery.

One wonders what would an artist
have done with Dachau gas ovens
or the bakeries of Buchenwald—
and such unquantifiable differences:
The Nazis' victims often were force-marched
to fates too inhumane for humanity to forget;
Southerners' slaves were worked typically
till old age, their bondage, we were taught
in grade school to believe, benevolent:

Symmetry.   Serenity.   Slavery.

Lenten Meditation

Wednesday of the smudge,
and I with forehead
more unblemished than soul
make the supreme sacrifice
of giving up nothing:
to roam for forty days,
carrying no cross
to cover my nakedness
and foregoing
this sacred serendipity of spring;
to walk in the wilderness
of total self-indulgence—
understood only by God

A Passion Play

(Scene: Appomattox Court House, Palm Sunday 1865)

In the troubled privacy of a tattered tent,
General Lee got off his knees and knew
what he must do to please a wrathful God.
Even in the darkness before dawn,
a true leader can see that destiny
may be delayed but not denied.

The rebel spirit which had soared
over Fort Sumter was at last subdued.
Defeat was a fact, surrender imminent,
capitulation as certain as any prophecy of Isaiah.
Among the Confederate troupers assembled
at Appomattox, only pride had survived intact,
a pride that had ever denied the inevitable,
a pride that had never permitted rehearsal
of the passion play about to begin.

The curtain rose on Palm Sunday,
a circumstance some suppose to be coincidence.
The site's natural scenery was right:
      gentle hills,   open fields,   a wood
filled with blossoming dogwood,
and here and there a split rail fence.
Awaiting a cue from Lee were the relatively few
surviving players he was about to surrender
in order to save their lives
even if it broke their hearts.
They were as grey as what they wore.
In the wings with Grant were several times as many
players in less tattered costumes of blue.
They held rifles and sabers,
guidons and battle flags, too.

When the proverbial cast of thousands was in place
and the only props missing were palm fronds,
Lee, the leading man in this real-life drama,
rode in, not on a never-ridden-before donkey,
but not cocky either,
just too proud to be too humble.

Millions have been moved by this image
of a man at the heart of their history,
and well into another century
curtain calls continue, reviewers rave
wherever Southern is spoken

The Tornadoes Next Time

A week after a dozen
devastating tornadoes struck this state,
another squall front moved
over Montgomery with the fury
normal for April in Alabama;
but when hail came
as if Heaven were a kingdom
of ice
breaking away bit by bit,
the faithful among us quivered,
remembering God's wreckage
the week before,
and saw it as a sign
that His rainbow promises
do not preclude
His wrath by wind

Wine, *Wild Flowers*, and West Virginia

The "Welcome to Wild, Wonderful West Virginia"
was a sincere sign your smile confirmed.
It greeted me at a vague border
between two states of compatible affection.

It presaged the path of least resistance
we chose to see your secret place,
reached by a woodsy walk beside a stream.
The walk had become a run
when a waterfall gave reason to rest.

Wine and music of *Wild Flowers*
combined as aphrodisiac to us,
and what followed was at least as lovely
as if it had been spontaneous.

We hallowed a hillside spot
beneath trees tall and tolerant,
while whispering of returning someday
to repeat this sweet indiscreetness.

You voiced then an endearing thought:
To find this Eden again,
you would have to crawl on your back
over all the lonely hills of wild,
wonderful West Virginia,

but that you would do it gladly
to come once more to place a plaque
proclaiming how this hill became sacred
to Venus in an Appalachian spring

July Poem

Susan awakening.
Sweet at midday.
Distance
in eyes belying
self-imposed poise.
Thoughts of something and someone
a hemisphere
and generation away,
out of sight of light blue eyes
seeing only distance.

Late day Susan,
at play on the strand.
Pebbles and toes.
Susan tanned and windblown lovely.

Susan going into the night
with the scent of blue grass
on wrists and elbows.

Susan and I beside the sea.
Yesterday.
Susan and I separated
by a dozen years
and society's ideas
about propriety.

Susan and I.
Someday

September Poem

Maybe
it's a futile wish
that we could have met this September
            instead of last September,
or that I could have had this year's maturity
            a year ago.

For
this year's maturity
doesn't even allow me to resent
            your having been wiser;
it only makes me regret
mistaking your wisdom for mere sophistication.

Now,
the melancholy season
finds me unready
            for its loneliness—
as unready as I was for you
            a year ago.

Soon,
when autumn leaves
take their predestined fall,
branches won't be the only things they bare;
something beneath my facade
            of sufficiency without you
will also be exposed

The Rites of Thanksgiving

The air is scented with anticipation.
The place of feasting is prepared
with fair linen and lit candle.
It is almost like an altar.
> *God is great; God is good.*

I take my place and, Pilgrimlike,
pause in praise of the nourishment
I am about to receive,
forgetting for the moment
all other blessings.
> *And we thank Him for our food.*

I salivate over the beautiful
beast before me as the beast within me
awakes and raises its head in hunger.
> *By His hands*

I begin by nibbling slowly
at a couple of cranberries,
simultaneously tart and sweet,
and sampling white meat of the breast.
> *we must be fed.*

I cover my hostess with compliments,
then progress to the dark,
meditating upon the juices.
> *Thank you, Lord,*

I take some of everything
and enter completely into
the spirit of the occasion.
> *for our daily bread.*

> *Amen.*

Carolina Sands

I return to Carolina sands
only in December now,
when winter's days
are windy and short—
each, like me, a refugee
        seemingly seeking refuge
                from the sea,
but hardly receiving warm welcome
    from the sullen sand
        where only pelicans walk,
                unconcernedly talking pelican talk,
as briny tides ebb and flow,
        washing away the heart prints
    we left there
                summers ago.

Do you recall?
Or perhaps you'd prefer not, after all
we're cosmopolitan now:
I've moved to the capital;
you're making the Broadway scene.

Somehow, however,
I think you'd remember
—if you allowed yourself—
why you flew out of the past
last November to surrender
                yourself
        —if even for a single night.

Your coming had some quality
that removed it from the realm of drama
and allowed it to become
the belated climax
our love should've had, but did not,
                              on Carolina sands
                                 summers ago

Carolina Sands II

These sands shall not feel my feet again
for I have learned not to fight fate.
I accept reality and turn
from this murky mirror termed Atlantic,
abandoning my search for solace
in its reflection of what might have been.

I shake the sand from my shoes
and leave the strand deserted
for the moment it takes seafowl
and fiddler crabs to reestablish their sovereignty.

> *Had I been Dafydd,*
> *I might have beckoned*
> *some gliding sea gull*
> *to inform you of a lingering love,*
> *but neither are you Morfudd*
> *—nor Carolina gulls Welsh.*

Yet, as I move inland, I know
this terminal pilgrimage had meaning
in occasioning the seaside prayer
said for you and your new love,
as I stooped to write
    in the sand
    a final poem,
    a one-word effort
    worth a thousand pictures:
    your name

A Long Way from New Orleans

Stirring, this morning, from sleep
too solitary to comfort,
I awoke to a world so newly white
outside my window, it seemed right
to linger in bed in reverie of you,
(white being your favorite absence of color)
reliving our loving in another season
in a crescent-shaped city of romance
far south of here, far south
where snow is rare and the newness
of our nearness was sufficient to warm us
long after we had to say goodbye.

I have promised to return someday
to take a lonelier walk along that levee,
low over the river,
where we were so high on each other.
I will go some night when the moon,
which is your mother, is bright enough
to shed some light on the mystery
that is the Mississippi in each of us.

And, if I feel like talking while I'm walking,
I will find a compassionate pelican
to tell how beautiful you were
traipsing barefoot down Bourbon Street
the night we opened oysters for hours
and took in *The Ginger Man*,
forgetting all our cares
in The City Which Care Forgot.

But tonight to find you,
I will take sight through my telescope
set up outside on the settled snow and,
peering through light years of cold winter air,
forgetting your sign was ever Cancer,
seek your face a long way from New Orleans,
seek it among the prettier Pleiades
forever

Winter Tree

Remembering the beauty
that was yours in other seasons,
I returned to lonely park today
seeking the solace of your summer shade.
But now I find your spring children
                              have
                         all
                              fallen
                                    away,
leaving your gnarled body and twisted

              limbs

too barren to comfort.
You have no solace to offer, winter tree,
and you can take none from lonely   me

Winter Song

Acclimated by an autumn long and lovely
enough to let us expect endless Indian summer,
we were ill-prepared last night
for winter's wrathfully sudden arrival
in the frozen form of severe ice storm.

Preoccupied with need for each other,
we were not ready to see a harsh reality:
the end of a season of serendipity.
We were not ready to see the limbs
of pines hanging limply
and miles of utility lines lying grounded,
as useless as self-centered love.
We were not ready to see the boundaries
of our egos collapsed.

Today we survey the damage,
contemplate its rearrangement
of the landscape of our lives.
We are sobered by the sight of so much
deceptively beautiful desolation.
Our happiness to have survived
is tempered by empathy, it seems,
with those whose hopes froze in the night
of burst pipes, broken hearts, dashed dreams.

In a milder afternoon of mid-December,
we remember and seek out a seasonal Messiah,
take refuge amidst its hallelujahs.
In this setting so ecstatic we are reminded
of Ecclesiastes and find solace
in Solomon's promise of a season for everything:
Just as sure as winter's time has come,
true love is as inevitable as next spring

Perennial

In summer, you said,
I'd taste the sea in you.
Nag's Head
would never be more
than an embrace away.

Autumn
would drive us to the Blue Ridges.
You'd draw, I'd write.
After art,
we'd alight on a bed
of gold, red,
and yellow foliage.

Winter
would find you singing
to me in front of fire,
bringing me in from the cold
every night.

In spring
we'd plant seed,
enough to satisfy our need
for regeneration.
In celebration we'd raise
strawberries and praise
the Source

Carolina Rose

As a young man,
more gallant than gardener,
I sowed my share of wild oats,
seldom lingering for the flower,
never waiting for the harvest.

Today, I pay the price
of my misplaced priorities
as the folly of so many fallow seasons
catches up with me and confronts me
upon seeing one special rose
I loved as a bud,
a thornless treasure I watered once
as precipitously as a summer shower,
then left in the care of a careless sharecropper
who was more at home with wild flowers,
sea oats.

Somehow it survived his abuse and abandonment,
and grew to maturity in the hands
of a more compassionate caretaker.

For a moment bittersweet with memory,
pregnant with possibilities uprooted long ago,
I watch this new gardener husband
his prize plant,
my soul souring with envy
as green as his thumb.

To act on that envy, of course, would be a crime
against nature and just in time
I subdue it, wish new caretaker well,
cast furtive glance at perfect rose,
flee his Garden of Eden, its treasure,
its temptation,
forever

Summer Swimmer

All winter, I've sensed a stranger within my skin.
By winter's end, I am withered.
The cold can force withdrawal of the flesh,
but after the everlasted winter
I begin to swim again.
The fluids of virility are thawed and flowing.

I

All winter, I've sensed a stranger within my skin,
a phantom whose form my fingers cannot feel.
These ten have lost touch with my toes,
and arms know legs no longer.
I suffer the syndrome of sedentary life.

II

By winter's end, I am withered
within the heavy shell of seasonal tweeds
and fur from soles to scalp.
I do not know how some survive in year-long snow:
The Eskimo is enigma to me.

III

The cold can force withdrawal of the flesh
from the warmest things in life.
When bodies are bundled up for frigid nights,
the cold can cause deferral of conjugal duties
and denial of conjugal rights.

IV

But after the everlasted winter,
there is a space of summer:
It is my season and I greet it by stripping
away every thread of cold-weather lethargy.
I encumber my trunk only with trunks.

V

I begin to swim again
and winter's slough is washed away
easier than a snake can shed its skin.
Hostilities between organs and outer parts
come to an end and I am whole.
My reunified body is free to seek its peace.

VI

The fluids of virility are thawed and flowing.
They transform me from winter's frog
into a tiger of the sea.
The forgotten breast stroke,
front crawl, elementary back
are recalled, are rejoiced again

Grandfather

Under his white crown of age,
grandfather had all the answers;
to us he was like a sage.

Now, he's silent
and we grandchildren ask only
the eternal question:
"Why did he die?"

Mothers too are wise,
and ours answered,
"Because God needed
another angel."

First Wife

We honeymooned at the shore,
deciding to spend the whole summer by the sea.
For months we were intimate enough
to monitor each other's every move.
The files of my mind filled
with the raw material of literature.

Then your departure came
like the shock of amputation,
and I forgot every creative ambition.
My days were spent in fruitless searches
along every East Coast strand
for a face that even resembled yours;
at best, the nights passed in fitful rest.

Finally, the approach of winter
ended my beachcombing,
and late last night, long after
city sounds ceased to distract,
I began (again) the definitive
life story of our love,
but still found it difficult to write
with your memory bending
over my shoulder

For a Lost Son

Happy birthday, son,
wherever you are.
Now you're 4.

I contested your adoption—
only in California could it happen—
lost you anyhow
because I'm so poor.

I wonder if your mommy and new daddy,
who could buy a boy as easily as a boat,
will let you keep the surname
that is your birthright.

But, what's in a name?
Blood counts for something,
sonny of mine,
and ours is the same

To A Red-Haired Exorcist

I perspire and find the heat no hardship.
The unrelieved hot nights and hot nuts
of Carolina childhood conditioned me
to great expectations of adulthood.

Baptism by total immersion
did not drown the horny devils
I wrestled through puberty,
demons who tempted me

with beautiful fantasy
at the risk of going blind.
The penalty if I lost
was eternity in darkness.

If I won, my reward
was sweated-out frustration.
So I chose to view the world
through sunglasses of fundamentalism,

and celebrated chastity
to the verge of bursting—
only then exchanging vows and virginities
with a nice girl next door:

an unequal exchange for each of us.
She would have been happier
with a eunuch,
I with a whore.

While we played house and groped
in the darkness of our experience
for missing precedents,
our summer honeymoon eclipsed quickly.

In the umbra of separation
I found solace in a passage
remembered from the writings of Saint Paul
about all things working together . . . .

In autumn of another year
I migrated to a free state and found
someone with bewitchingly long red hair
—and needs like my own

Washington, D.C.

Potomac island
in the mainstream of America,
an epitome of human diversity,
site of the Federal conglomeration,
scene of scarred streets
and cherry-blossomed trees,
but it's more than all these—

Washington,
more than a capital.

Washington,
geographic center
of my emotions

Dinner Candles

sharp reflections
        seconds ago
diffused now
shining beacons of affection
          in moist eyes
          crying out to me
                        your love

sharp reflections
        wounding always
        wounds that never heal

reflected wounds
        always soothed
         by your tenderness
         softly diffused

Second Genesis

Through a trinity of seasons
you, my babe, enjoyed an Eden
uniquely yours; and restless now
in artificial womb still
isoletted from unsterile world,
you sense its absence only
groggily, not yet knowing
that you have forgotten all
the knowledge ancestrally acquired
over eons in your birthfall
through all the generations.

Later you may miss that garden
from which ever consistent,
endlessly repetitious Nature,
heedless of embryonic bliss,
has summarily expelled you;

but now you are too busy to care,
having already found countless
fingers and toes and beginning
again a long life of re-learning

New Life

Gurgling
at your fountain of youth,
close to the heart
whose beat was once your own,
even your coos
speak the contentment
of a new life impured
only by the sins of your fathers;
but you bring hope even to them,
dear daughter,
and yours
is like a second coming

New Priorities

My preoccupation
is no longer empires;
I tiptoe in darkness
to witness your blanket's
rise and fall.
Then,
bending over the slats of your crib
that remain silent sentries
through the night,
I become reacquainted with a God
I knew in my youth
and say a wordless prayer
of hope for your future,
which is the future of all the world,
while listening
for the sweetest sound I have ever heard:
your breathing

Mother's Day

(written on behalf of an infant daughter)

This is your day and I,
swaddled in your favorite hue,
am like a little pink rose
plucked from within you.

This is your day—and I,
the fruit of your love for another,
a turtledove of your hearts,
am glad he's my dad, you my mother!

This is your day—and I,
cute as a duckling and cuddly too,
tiny shoot of taller tree,
hear your sigh and coo

the contentment of being me

Two Years At Kitty Hawk

1968

On sands granulated
from dunes where once Wrights flew
and Frost walked and wrote,
we made our own discoveries:
>   yours, the distance
>   of my distraction;
>   mine, the tears that stung
>   more than salt spray.

1969

This year we'll retrace
as one the separate
steps imbedded in the sand
of uncovered memory.
We shall view the same barren
beauty with new vision
and share our daughter's
delight at the sight
>   of the sea

Outer Banks Explanation

Now my suffering is salty,
relief geographic.
I have found what others
have sought to discover:
the skinny enigma, Kitty Hawk.

Its meaning may be life,
multiplied by humanity,
migrated from the sea,
moving again to its edge
for reunion with earliest origin.

I see it tied like a long lifeboat
between capes of solace;
I see it climbed upon by some
hoping to find themselves,
and others with purpose lost in custom.

It means for me a returning
    to sleep under stars and not be afraid,
    to slumber on sand with no midnight awakening
                    to write *Croatan.*

It means returning
    to dream unbroken dreams across somniferous nights,
    making love like Adam, seen only by God
                    and Eve.

It means
    to awake at first light with a face full of sun.

It means returning
    to beginning

Destination Dublin

The Empire State twinkles
and fades from sight;
the universe is dark
except for points of light
                in the heavens.

Upward   upward   fixed wings soar
leaving earth and sound behind.
Eastward   eastward   sweeping silently
toward celestial beacons blinking white.

Eastward   eastward   racing to meet
the sun by slicing the night in half.
Faster   faster   making miles
minute and minutes go backwards.

We trespass through lairs of bears,
major and minor, then cross
a backyard of seven sisters,
a vacuum of no resistance.

Within, sealed from sound but not sight,
eyes widen, then linger with more love
than those of astronauts, whose view
could not fulfill more than quilted
patterns greeting pilgrims in reverse.

Hearts quicken as wheels screech
on the dawn of new lives;
emotions swell into poems, and I smile,
realizing I have broken
the brown bag of my existence

46

Lucca

In
a house
named "Lucca"
out from Dublin
On Coliemore Road,
we renewed an old love
for the ever constant sea.
We found what we sought: a fresh start
upon the ashes of yesterday,
a Hibernian holiday to clear
a poet's mind of civil service morass;
here we found a clear window on life, below which
the surf pounds ancient rocks with invigorating sounds
and through which rays of new days bring inner brightness
that by night appears as a lighthouse blinking
in the center of my brain, messages
of inspiration in red Morse code:
"Write about what you see and feel;
this is purest poetry."
So now I write these scenes
and sounds in the now
Irish archives
of my mind—
preserved,
pure

At Trinity College

In Trinity's front square
I rest companionless
beside the Campanile.
My gaze goes up to a blue-faced clock
which seems to say
it is half-past my life;
it goes down as if to search
for the years of my lost youth.
I wonder how I could have grown
        so old
without ever once holding hands
with a Celtic beauty
in the basement Buttery.

I have watched sex stalk this campus
in every shape and size,
petite girls pointedly
putting their best fronts forward,
bulge upon bulge beneath sweaters
of all sensual colors,
taller girls stretching trim legs forever.

I have coveted in secret
these products of eighteen or more
years of Irish milk and exercise,
dreaming of Deirdres, Mauves,
and a Nuala I may never know.
But I am no *Ginger Man*—
my lust must not touch them.
My projected major is monogamy

Rendezvous in Reykjavik

The shortest distance between
two lovers being a rendezvous,
we have met in Reykjavik
to discover the birthplace
of the discoverers of our birthplace.

Crossing sea and glacier, you come
with Trinity's colors to warm my neck;
I arrive from America confessing
your new meaning to me.

Thus, our mid-North Atlantic meeting
in the land of noonday night
achieves even deeper meaning:
our discovery of each other.

We explore a week of honeyearth
in this lunar-landscaped escape,
finding beauty in desolation,
saddened only by the thought
of its crumbling away
into an uncaring ocean.

Here we reach a higher
plateau of affection,
and can return now
                 To Ireland, with Love

Rhythm Method

Without a doubt, I have
seen this devout nation's
wonders from windows of
the Dalkey to Dublin bus
more authentically
than foreign takers of
ten thousand packaged tours.

And forever framed in my
memory of Dun Laoghaire
will be a weary young wife,
still stylish and healthy
in life's prime,
dutifully pramming her son—
he, hardly a year old;
she, burdened by shopping bag
and Catholic bulge
beneath bountiful breasts

Charity

Never so carefree
as Liffey gulls
lilting above crossers
of O'Connell Bridge,
at mid-river a ragged child,
squatting on the *Irish Times*,
begs of passersby
congratulating themselves
on being wise
to her game

After Inniskeen

Semi-hypnotized by windshield
wipers' ceaseless semi-circles,
my eyes follow an April-showered
T-2 winding south from Inniskeen
where I have just been to pay homage
to Patrick Kavanagh and found
my father there—no, not in body,
but in the spirit of one remembered
at the grave of another—
and as Monaghan falls behind
I see it in the rear view mirror
of my mind, remaining as it has
been for decades: green fields
and gentle hills fully fertile
for a poetry often lived,
                    yet rarely written.

Monaghan falls behind as Dublin
comes nearer, and as the sky
becomes clearer over this same road
the late blooming bard traveled
in search not of escape from his great
hunger, but of its fulfillment, I

                pray for
                him
            who walked
                apart
            on the hills
            loving life's
            miracles

a grateful token silently spoken
for helping me discover
the poetry of his unknown
contemporary, my own father, Paul,
who, perhaps, unlike Patrick,
never forgot that print on paper
doesn't matter, wrote his not in books
but on leaves of life in sweat and tears.

Now I with more than much to learn
try to exhume his unwritten lines.
Paul shall be published vicariously
while Patrick's reputation remains
unchallenged, his philosophy re-vindicated.

In spring of 1970
Paul and Patrick are silent.
Again, the days become longer.

A leaf floats beneath Baggot Street Bridge
on a greater journey than I have ever dreamed—
it does not care

Famine

*A curate at Ballyfermot in Dublin last night charged
the community and Dublin County Council with
responsibility for the death of a three-month-old itinerant
child, Sarah Donaghue, from pneumonia in Cherry
Orchard Hospital on Saturday night.*

*The Donaghue family, said Fr. Con O'Keefee, had
been living in a broken-down van on the roadside after
being bulldozed out of their original home—a wooden hut
in a nearby field—about two weeks ago.*

The Irish Press
February 1, 1971

Little Sarah had no place to lay her sleepy head
although, so it's said, there are in Dublin
many Georgian mansions emptier than the hearts
of her Ballyfermot neighbors who bulldozed
her family's simple home into splinters
without giving as much as a tinker's damn.

Maybe Council thinks mansions too dear for itinerants
who cannot pay rents even on rotten tenements.
In any case, exposure followed eviction,
and in its damp chill little Sarah fell ill
with more pneumonia than her frail body could bear.
Within a fortnight her suffering was finished.

Now little Sarah is dead; only her hunger goes gnawing on.
At first it was thought she had died in her own fluids,
but an autopsy held by Celtic Twilight
established cause of death as apathy
to the plight of itinerants everywhere,
a fearsome malignancy known in other lands by other names.

After Requiem Mass Sarah's mourners wondered what were
her last delirious dreams in Cherry Orchard Hospital—
a regret that she would never grow big enough to beg
on O'Connell Bridge or solicit coppers on St. Stephen's Green?
Did she hear angels calling "*Céad Míle Failte* to Heaven,
little cherub. Rejoice and have no fear"?

Tomorrow when her death certificate comes through the G.P.O.,
(the storied scene of modern Ireland's finest hour)
Cuchulain's statue will shudder in shame
and Ballyfermot land values shall soar—
what with one less tinker living next door.
An old cliche could then be revised and restated:
"People who live in stone houses
should never toss glass potatoes."

The Untied Kingdom

No longer so united,
the transposition of even
a single "i" can untie it.

No matter how royally loud the roar
of its lion, any political entity
is only as durable as its dignity.

Pomp becomes pathetic,
depraved boasts of never-setting suns
deserve one's everlasting reproach.

Now history confirms how this
anachronism grew as fat as its figureheads
on the pickings of imperialism

decade after bloody decade
as it vultured itself into decadence
and obesity reigned.

The kingdom has found itself finally,
bound by dark knights of diminished vision
and dismal days of diminished might;

but imperial pride dies slowly
and persists in bullying an ancient foe
which refuses to stay vanquished

Ditty for St. Patrick's Day

Today I'm wearin' the green
and I've sent to the Queen
a resignation of my English ancestry.
To be sure, I'd rather be honorary Irish,
livin' with the truly free,
than to have the sickly red lion
—dyin'—
in my family tree.

Filial

My mother's world has lost its balance
and spins in new directions so fast
her equilibrium cannot follow.
Her walk becomes a wobble in the spin-off
which also carries away her memory
and I am called by my brother's name,
                     he by mine.

Still, pride is paramount
and does not permit the use of a prescribed cane.
She refuses to learn to walk again.

Forgetting the limitations
years have imposed upon her limbs,
she tries to lift an already too heavy
two-year-old granddaughter from a stroller,
only to see her loving kindness cause a fall
at the bottom of which skin stretched thin
by old age is met by unyielding steel.

Then, as the failing vision of faded eyes
is revived momentarily by flashing stars of every color,
her blue and white striped dress becomes patriotic
with the red appearance of her blood.

I am summoned not by her silence,
but by my child's bewildered cry.
Stunned by this scene into immobility,
I am able only to seek the assistance
of Samaritan neighbors adept in first aid.

Afterwards, a rushed ride the wrong way
down a one-way street gets us to a physician
where her silk stockings are swapped for silk sutures.

I watch and flinch with the pain of sympathy
as I see sewn the legs that bear the body that bore me.
I hold her hand consolingly to soothe
the deeper pain of embarrassment and say,
"Don't cry, Mother. Everything will be all right."

Tribute to a Matriarch

You should wear your years
like stars in a crown, Gram,
(They look so grand in grey!)
or ribbons decorating a soldier's chest.

Time is a shroud
which will wrap each of us soon enough;
it need not be as well
an ultimate albatross
to bend ancestral necks.

Your loving longer than any of us
is challenge to a worthy goal:
to grow old so gracefully.

Thinking of these things on Christmas Eve,
and of you in a place where there
is nurture but no nativity,
your granddaughter, her husband, and child
travel far to fetch you home.

Returning to the gathering clan
with familial gift more precious
than gold or frankincense or myrrh,
they follow in spirit the star
that led the Magi from the East

To My Second Wife

I

There is a Baptist preacher
in the background of my mind.
From his "until death do us part" pulpit,
he declares divorce a sin.
I believed him until a final decree
forced for me the cruel choice:
continence or second spouse
slept with in continuing sin.
That is a God-damned fiction—
and damned are those who impose it
upon the God-fearing meek.
If Jesus loves me, I should be free
to seek renewal in remarriage
and to pursue the possibilities
of salvation from fates far worse
than theological sin.
In Heaven souls may be content
not to screw around,
but on Earth the burden of the body
is too great to bear alone.
The promise of forever is tentative
where affairs of human hearts
are concerned.
We have learned the hard way
it is a sacred contract
which must be renegotiated daily.

II

Let me say what this second chance
means to me:
It is a kind of trust
and a kind trust in each other.
We have lived sixteen seasons together—
and this is a lifetime
or a moment gone too quickly.

We should measure time
by heartbeats in unison
or by the depths of our delight
in each other.
I know I have used that phrase before
and I will try again to say
what this means to me:
Today I enjoyed the therapy
of temporary separation.
I remembered September with sadness
only because I had not loved you enough.
Now I live with the hope of October:
that we not think of this month
in terms of ten or as an ending
but just as the beginning
of four more seasons to test together.

To dwell on this talk of seasons
may be silly, although I always think
of loving you as like having
a bit of summer sunshine
to warm any kind of winter.

But think of it, think of it!
This is greater
than the promise of "forever":

III
The first *luckenbooth*
I gave to you was lost.
So was my first marriage.
You and I, though, have found
significance in second chances.

Today is our fourth anniversary.
I give you now another
Scottish betrothal brooch
to wear until the coming
of our second child

Blue Robe

Lying awake, I await
your entry.
My position is that of rest,
but my attitude is anticipation.
You delay erotically with womanly preparation.
The shower has washed away foreign odor.
The brisk toweling has you tingling.
Spanish *Joya* is pressure pointed
to accent sensual natural scents.
You dress to be undressed.

Finally,
the door opens
and candle glow reveals
an image in blue.
In lacey white slippers you appear
to be stepping on clouds.
As graceful movement brings you closer,
your blue robe billows gently over hills, valleys, knolls
I know well from intimate exploration.
Yet,
I am amazed again to be approached
by this beatific figure—not an apparition,
for you are flesh and blood as well as soul and love.

Initial contact is electric, but does not kill.
Moist lips meet and linger together.
My fingers tease through long red hair,
yours among the growth on my chin and chest.
We climb a peak
as ecstatic

as Mount Sinai,
then comes the moment of religious experience,
my offering to the burning bush
and a new psalm:
Love one another;
this must be why God made us as He did.
Love one another.

Fulfilled,
we remain as close as Siamese twins,
belly-joined,
to greet the morning's joy

A Loaf of Love

All day long
our kitchen has been warmed
by your baking of bread;
I, by the electric heat
you radiate too, when making things
(as well as non-things).
I sense this receptivity
to be reciprocal
and try to pry you away
from the kitchen,
playfully protesting
the false economy of home-baked bread.
Your aproned embrace admits
what was said about man
not living by it alone,
and adds, "Yes, it's a labor of love."
So, I stand at your heels
with the strained patience
of simmering desire
to watch you knead the dough.
Put aside, it rises
while we no longer wait
to satiate our hungers.
You feel my own need
as you open the oven
to insert the dough.
It continues to rise,
to rise and get bigger . . .
until the buzzer

A Pregnant Woman

turns her back
to the man
who has ruined
her figure;
too full to face him,
her turning is to receive,
not reject,
his loving

To A New Son

Welcome to life, little boy,
yours and mine.
Your joyful presence is all
the vindication we need
for the impulsively sown
seeds of last June.
My role in its beginning
was one I relished
with regret only
that I am not the Father
who can give you it eternal.
Rest assured,
as we share awhile
the lovely joy
of your mother's breasts,
that she and I shall care for you always.
We do not feed you mother's milk
to make you fatter cannon fodder.

While the coming of children
and passing of years
have not made me pacifist,
I have become much more choosy
about accepting alternatives
to peace.
Mothers and fathers of the world
may never learn
to live without war,
but the coming of each new child
gives us another chance.

I believe in children

Have Faith and Wait

(for Paul & Joseph Anthony)

I

My son Joseph grows toward manhood
with another man's name
in another country far away.
The many-colored coat of his youth
has never brightened my eyes.
I do not know why we're kept apart,
though I did not sell him
and would pay any price for his presence.
> *Joseph, I'm told there must be famine*
> *before the feast of reunion.*
> *Until then you should serve your pharaoh*
> *with proper deference.*
> *When you become the governor*
> *of your own life,*
> *the famine will end.*

II

My faith in a god who loves men
as well as women and children
has been vindicated:
My waiting has wrought a new son.
> *You, Paul, are all the sons*
> *I have never known*
> *and all the sons I shall ever know.*
> *You are the son of all fathers before*
> *and shall be the father of all sons after.*

> *Paul, you are yourself*
> *and your father's father reborn*
> *in name if not flesh.*
> *Your ancient namesake held the latter*
> *to be of lesser importance anyway.*

I know boys need brothers
and, if you were of age, Paul,
I would bid you seek your own,
a boy named Joseph growing toward manhood
in another country far away.

But you are yet too small
and I too blind to find the way.
Our Joseph will come home
when be is grown.
Paul, have faith
and wait with me

Sandbox

From a seaport in the Southeast
a night flight streaks
toward the City of Steel.
Four of the passengers aboard
are my family and me.
I have just treated us
to a weekend in my hometown
where a million camellias bloomed
as a reminder
of its earlier spring.
In the seat beside me
sleeps a bundle of blonde exhaustion.
Several hours ago, she frolicked
in the warm waters
of "Folly the Beach,"
a joyous spendthrift
with the energy she was unable to use
during the long winter of western Pennsylvania.

While you dream,
my beloved daughter,
of a sandbox the length of the Atlantic,
I pray our journeys homeward
won't always be away from the sea

The Words

It is halfway between four
and five in the morning,
for most of the world
an hour of sleep
as night changes to half-light,
metamorphosing itself into day.

It is an hour of sleep,
but I am wide-awake,
a room and hallway away from my bed,
from the waiting warmth of sleeping spouse,
another room away from the blonde solace
of sleeping son,
a world away from everyone,
in the lonely early morning
world of the writer.

Outside, the wind drives by in a noisy truck
every few minutes,
back and forth,
back and forth.
Inside, the only sounds are the scratches
I make on paper
as, with pen in pensive hand,
I stab for an elusive poem in the back of my brain,
somewhere back there behind my consciousness
waiting more patiently than I
for the birth canal of creativity to dilate.

It is an hour of sleep,
and I struggle in this lonely labor alone,
utterly, painfully alone,
until the small body of a boy appears
beside my chair and, without waiting for invitation,
perches upon my lap.
He leans back as if to continue his night's nap,
his head over my heart,
his blonde hair soft beneath my chin,
and the emotions begin to flow,
the feelings which are the forerunners
of those wonderful words called poetry.
*   *   *
Paul, you wonderful son,
full of joy and wonder,
I wonder about you
and why you came.
I wonder about your genesis
and wonder if I caused your mother
to conceive you
or if you, perceiving my loneliness
for a lost son
through the many layers of freckles, skin, flesh, muscle
which lay over the egg of your earlier existence,
came into the world of your own accord to comfort me.

Paul, I wonder about you,
perched upon my lap,
your head over my heart,
your blonde hair soft beneath my chin,
perceiving all that is joyful between father and son:
this moment is ours,
this moment which is our life
which is only a moment in time

which we cannot slow
but only stop for as long as we love
and which, if the words are right,
we can stop for as long as our words are read.

Paul, perched upon my lap,
your head over my heart,
your blonde hair soft beneath my chin,
Paul, perceiving all that is joyful between us,
because of you I am believing now that there is hope
for our lonely world,
for, if there is one like you,
there may be many like you,
willing to love,
wanting to love,
waiting to love other fathers.

So, you are not unique
except in your uniqueness,
and because you are Paul,
and because I love you because you are Paul
and not Ray or Michael or Joseph Anthony or Jeffrey
or any other little fellow,
who are all just as lovable,
who are all just as beloved by other fathers
who are all making the world what it is.

And the world at 4:30, Paul,
is a lonely place without you
perched upon my lap,
your head over my heart,
your blonde hair soft beneath my chin,
and the world would be a far worse place, Paul,
without you and those like you with other names

perceiving the loneliness of fathers everywhere,
fathers who are making the world what it is
and making it lonelier altogether too often
because they/we have forgotten how to love
as you do,
as you do so completely,
as you do with perception
and not precondition.

Paul, perched upon my lap,
your head over my heart,
your blonde hair soft beneath my chin,
Paul, perched and perceiving all that is
ultimately important to each of us,
to both of us,
to all of us,
Paul, the words are coming now,
the words,
the most wonderful words of the world,
the words,
the wonderful words of life, of love,
the words,
the wonderful words,
the words,
the words

Metaphors Be With You

Wrestling with words, laboring over lines,
I was immersed in my study
in the hard work of writing,
but, happily,
was not too busy to be bothered
with a little boy.
And you made my day,
Paul,
taking a moment from your play
and making it into a memory,
just by running into my room
and summoning me so excitedly:
"Daddy, Daddy, come see balloon!"
Although I knew, even at the age of two,
you were quite a tease (though not yet poet),
I wanted to please, and in jest
I rushed in your wake to a window facing west
just in time to see on distant trees
the soft settling
of a big bright, and beautiful
orange sun
—just like you metaphorically said,
Son

Weekend

There may be more poems never written
about New York than one would ever guess,
composed in no known meter or meaning
by multitudes mumbling in noisy streets.

At the Ides of February we crossed
the Alleghenies to be among
them for a day to lose ourselves
from everyone except each other,

but our going had a difference:
we went to write a Valentine
memorable in many ways,
found a single penny sufficient
to subsidize a child's candy-colored quest
for happiness and realized our own almost
impossible dream as the dreamer from La Mancha
danced before us with graceful company.

Yes, our going had a difference:
we knew better than to try to *live* there;
we only wanted to love there

Boxing Day on Tobago

Reeling from the steel drum
confusion and carnival color
of Christmas in Trinidad,
reeling from too much Island
rum and roast pig,
reeling from my disquieted wife's
suggestion of separation,
and feeling some psychic need
to spend a quiet day in the sun,
we arose early on the Feast of Stephen
to visit the smaller half
of this schizophrenic paradise,
flying to Tobago
through the cumulus clouds of the Caribbean,
the shadow of our plane
unprophetically encircled in a rainbow.

Touching down on the tranquility that is Tobago,
our Pennsylvania problems a thousand miles away,
we reached the bucolic beach
with a short walk from Scarborough Airport
and soon were swimming in shimmering sea.
Later we lay on sparkling sand,
hand touching hand as bodies burned
and faces tanned.
Later still we chartered a glass-bottomed boat
to see the splendor of Buccoo Reef.

That day of seaside serendipity
was our first in far too many months,
and much too late to save our marriage;
that day of semi-serenity
would be the last in the lifetime
of a sometimes idyllic union
supposed to last a lifetime.
That day like all days was finite,
and, when the sun was setting
on the other side of the Andes,
we descended into Port-of-Spain
for the final night of our holiday.
At dinner I ate slowly, prayed it would last,
that the night would be long
before it belonged to the past.

Later, in the damp tropical dark,
too tired to think of troubled future,
oblivious even to the present pain of sunburn,
we turned again toward each other
to consummate our Caribbean Christmas,
last legacy of a soon-to-be-lost love.

By dawn the steel drums were silent

Coffee and Solace

The sensation
is strange
fifteen minutes later
in a donut shop,
(It's not the *shop* that's strange.)
selecting
(Not without some difficulty.)
a vanilla donut
stuck on a stick
and small black coffee
to go,
(So what?)
and bringing forth the change
(Ah, the change!)
from my pocket
and finding in the center
of my palm
among the pennies, dimes, nickels
needed to pay the 43¢ tab
a woman's wedding band, gold,
so recently worn by my disenchanted wife.
(Shocking! But preferable, perhaps,
to being dismembered—unless, of course,
the reference is to one's psyche.)

Outside again,
the eve-of-April night
is cold,
the air flaked with snow.
(Typical unseasonable season.)
And on my way over an Allegheny mountain
(Up, up and away.)
I am glad to have the stimulating company
of this coffee,

this donut,
the solace of some memories
still too warm
to be chilled
by anything.
(coffee and solace?)

Sipping, munching,
I drive over the mountain:
Calm.   Lonely.   Older.

In the Land of Disenchantment

Putting most of the continent between us
was as naive as thinking
the world is flat:
Two thousand miles are not enough
to soothe the pain of loving you
unrequitedly.
(And, if New Mexico won't do it,
why would the moon?)

I know now the futility of seeking peace
in a place;
(No Santa Fe can be more than respite.)
the solace I crave comes from inner space.

And in the desert's dry night,
beneath a billion distant stars,
I also realize
that
neither is distance between places
the key to relief.
Were it otherwise,
I might think in terms
of the light years required
to move beyond the range
of every memory
of you

On Vacating a Condo in Reston, Virginia

CONDO FOR SALE. 1588 Moorings Drive,
Unit 12-C. Outside the Beltway but
within an easy hour's drive to downtown
D.C. 3 bedrooms w/ balconies, 2½
baths (too many now, as well as too much).
Lovely year-round views (depending
upon one's perspective)—seasonal
view of Lake Anne. Walk to Safeway,
schools, tennis, and pools.
Ironically but certifiably blessed by
ordained priest of the Episcopal Church.
Divorced owner eager to begin new
life in New Orleans has priced
at less than market for quick sale.
Rare opportunity to grab the brass ring
and do your thing in "Commuter City."
What was sometimes my purgatory,
sometimes my Parnassus,
can be your paradise all the time.
(Will even throw in a tricycle
my tot may be too big to ride
by the time he sees it again—
indeed, his mom's that mad!)
Immediate occupancy (if not sooner).
Call Eugene, 435-0220.

Final Decree

No divorce is ever final;
any decree to the contrary,
is merely a legal fiction.

Still, this fiction persists,
often at odds with reality,
the anguish of real life.

For two who truly have been one,
divorce is like pulling wisdom teeth
without anesthesia or, if anesthetized,
felt long after the pulling—
like the pain of phantom limb
severed from torso long ago.

What two human beings have wrought
by joining together, to have
and to hold in sickness and in health,
in the wealth of concord as well
as in the poverty of discord,
those demigods, the juris doctors of divorce,
should be enjoined to put asunder
until vulnerable clients can lie
sleepless enough lonely nights to change
their fickle minds

Machinist

Braving a thousand last mornings,
neither coward nor lazy, my father,
arising to die on the job,
watching his world's final revolutions
on a turning lathe
glistening with sweat dripping
from his machined features
and reflecting his grey

Pennies From Heaven

Robbed by emphysema
of outdoor passions,
my dad hobbied through
two years of retirement,
a new collector
of old coins.

Thus, my gift: the wealth
of thirty-eight cents,
a small tribe
of Indian Head Pennies,
tiny tokens of tribute,
remembrance for a final
Christmas—
given before he
took the ultimate reward
and left me the fortune
of having been his son

To Bury A Stranger

That which I have dreaded
    for so long
    now appears
    imminent.

It's inevitable
    —his doctor said—
    he might go
    at
    any
    moment.

Nothing—
    there's nothing
    for me to say
    or to think.

For there are no words or thoughts
    to express
    the anguish . . . the regret . . .
    the intensity of anguish and regret
    and the love
    I must feel . . . if I can feel

for this man
    who impregnated my seed
    before I was,

for this man
    who gave his life on the installment plan
    for my mother, my brother, and me,
    and before that
    for his own mother, brothers, and Thee.

O God,
     You know. You must know—
     Didn't Your son
     give Himself on the tree
     when He was only
     half as old as my daddy?

If You must take him now,
     please wait.
     Please wait at least
     until I can fly to his side
     and tell him tactful lies
     and make plans and promises
     that'll never be.

Don't take him
     before I can get there
     and kiss his hand
     and try to make him understand
     that I'm not ungrateful
     for the sacrifices
     that make and will always make
     my accomplishments his accomplishments.

Circumstances didn't allow him
    most of life's delights and dignities
    —like a high school diploma—
    and he never studied in Ireland
    or skied in Peru
    or did many of the things I want
    and plan to do.

I'm not even sure
    I know him
    we're so unalike.
    Please withhold Your call;
    give me another chance
    to get closer than acquaintance
    to my father Paul.

Don't make me
    bury
    a stranger

Flight 227

Flight 227 tearing down the runway
    45 minutes late
    45 minutes less chance
        to reach you

In a moment
    we'll be above broad avenues,
    memorials, monuments, cherry blossoms,
    landmarks familiar to me now
    in the city which pulled me
    from the place where you and Mom
    greeted my birth

Ears popping now
    gaining altitude
    getting closer
    a thousand feet per second
    getting closer
    getting closer to you, Pop,
    getting closer

"What will be, will be."
    I believe it
    I only hope
    Father Don's prayer
    won't let it be
    before I can get there
    to tell you
    you'll be all right

(What does one do
    on a dinner flight
    going to see
    perhaps to bury
    his old man

What shall I do
     on Flight 227
     slicing through April night
     a little lower than Heaven)

There's no need to write you, Dad.
     I think I sent
     the final letter
     two days ago special delivery
     with Christmas stamps.
     Did you receive it—
     before the coma

Maybe that doesn't matter either.
     Soon we can talk together anywhere,
     once you escape
     your wracked, exhausted body
     into the ether, into the air

There's Charleston's glow
     and your other son waiting for me
                    below
     We'll be with you in a minute, Dad.
     Wait for us

The Greatest Man

Dad, you didn't always dig
    the manner of hip expression.
This may be the final time
    I use this one:
"Man, you're the greatest!"
    —proving us all wrong—
and I'm the ashamedest son
    for having been one
of those who were ready
    to give up your ghost
before you were ready
    to leave your post
as head of the household,
    king of your five-room castle.
The experts gave you
    perhaps only hours,
but as the hours ticked away,
    your heart ticked with them.
You were the epitome
    of prostrate magnanimity.
Even from your adjustable bed,
    the concerns that filled your head
were for the adversities and ills
    of others.
You even allowed me
    to acquire humility
by putting you on the bed pan
    and wiping you
as you must have wiped me
    so often, so long ago.
I wanted to do more
    and offered to no avail a lung—

it was the least that I could do,
    and it was less,
less than a half-return for the two
    you had given me
and for the two you wore out
    for my college degree.
Your living has made all of us better,
    and we'll stick with you all the way—
all the way because . . .
    you're trying so very, very hard to stay.

"Man, you're the greatest!"

Transition

The need for ambulance speed
having become pointless with
his debilitating years,
we help my father slowly
from the bed he has shared with no one
for forty months, help him to his
automobile that will take him away
from his humble, homemade home
for the final time.
My brother drives down Orleans Road,
bordered by the budding trees
of a South Carolina spring.
We drive past houses of neighbors,
occupied mostly by widows, fewer widowers,
houses of friends whom my father
has outlived and of those who will outlive
my father.
But he does not look
for he knows it would be a last look
and prefers not to see them through dying eyes.
We proceed eastward on U.S. 17
past the outlets of our basic needs.
shopping centers and gasoline dealers,
a grocery store named *Piggly Wiggly*,
a Baptist church named for Ashley River.
Our only stops are two required by traffic lights
insensitive to the human condition,
and in less than an hour we arrive at Roper Hospital.
He has been here before—many times—but it still
is not like the home where his shirts and suits
remain hanging in a closet. Neckties knotted.
Shoes unworn for months gathering a little more dust.
It does not matter. He will not need them.
Hospital pajamas are the uniform of the day.

He is checked into a semi-private room
so that he will not die alone.
Ordered to rest, he refuses to sleep away
his last days and nights. I spend the first
of the last by his side. He is unable to speak
and I to keep up a one-way conversation.
I read aloud awhile from a book by a Greek
of whom he has never heard.
At last he feigns sleep to allow me rest.
The morning marks another day gone.
I stand aside then slip away
as a new shift of starched nurses
begin their routines

Message

I knew that someday
the message would come,
that someday my dad's days
would be done.
But, prodigal son far from home
and out of touch too long to know
his end was imminent,
I really wasn't ready
(when finally the call came)
for the cold incongruity
of being shown the terse note
while slumped in a dentist's chair,
nerves (but not emotions)
numbed by novocain
and my mouth so full
of prosthetic paraphernalia,
I could only sigh

The American Way

I wouldn't have recognized you
if I hadn't known,
if I had been merely passing through.

While you weren't the picture of health
during those last hospital days,
that stark reality was no worse
than what they did with excess cosmetics.

Looking at your body lying there
in its satin-lined, thousand-dollar
                    flip top box,
I realize better than ever
why I too detest
            the American way of going
                to eternal rest

Prayer

NOW I LAY ME DOWN TO SLEEP
like most of my life's other nights
in this house which you built
with your own hands
but this is the first time I'll sleep in it
while you weren't sleeping or awake—somewhere

NOW I LAY ME DOWN TO SLEEP
thinking about tomorrow's duty
to lay you down
in the earth to keep

NOW I LAY ME DOWN TO SLEEP
hoping that I won't think about the things
that brought tears to my eyes today
and to my lips once the cry "God . . ."
as I was speeding on my way
(You wouldn't have approved—I really sped!)
to see you off
on this fantastic voyage
you've embarked upon

NOW I LAY ME DOWN TO SLEEP
    IF I SHOULD DIE BEFORE I WAKE
Oh, no, for Christ's sake—only one of us at a time,
please!
Let me stay for a while
to tend his grave
and give substance to any final wishes
he may have made

NOW I LAY ME DOWN TO SLEEP

The Last Ride

It's your big day, Dad.
  You'll head the procession
    as we go Cadillacin'
      —with police escort, no less—
        to that little plot you bought in the country
          among the trees.
            It'll be a coat 'n tie affair
              (By the way, we had your suit cleaned
                and bought you a new shirt.)
                  People'll be coming
                    from far and near
                      to pay you tribute.
                        (They haven't been through it.)
                          It's time to go now,
                            this must cease.
                              In closing, let me say
                                I'll miss you—
                                  and rest in peace

News Bulletin:

Edinburgh doctors
perform Europe's first
lung transplant.

(seventeen days too late, Dad,
                  to be of interest
                  to you)

That's No Way to Say Goodbye, Tammy

I

There's no honor,
respite or solace
beating my head
against the stone wall
of your disenchantment;
but my sense of loss
is being assuaged now
by an angry annoyance with myself
for having hung around
puppy dog like
for a few more kicks
in the heart.

II

The Little Prince,
precious story,
bittersweet ending.

Your giving it
as a final gift
was very like you.

(But I put it aside
and finished reading it
the night my father died.)

Visitation Rights

The winters of upstate New York
are long, but never last till June.
The snow which closed your school today,
a school I've never seen, I'm sorry to say—
this snow shall melt and soften earth,
promote the growth of fantastic forms
of life in yellow, green, and white.

One sun-filled morning sometime soon,
allow yourself to wake and see
the first forsythia of spring
and beneath budding trees the tracks
of a unicorn a lot like you.

Way down here in South Carolina,
where snow and unicorns are rare,
it's always winter without you—
I count the days until you come
for the month we await all year

On the Beach

Grey met grey that sunless day,
the air and sea so cold
the gulls froze in flight.
We shivered in storm-swept sand
and longed for the night
when by marshmallow fire's light
we could write on the wind.
but seaside fantasy is born
to die in tides of reality

At last in the lee of a dune
we found warmth in the closeness
of inches we knew would remain
a final barrier forever.
but seaside fantasy is born
to die in tides of reality

In the marshmallow glow
imagination was re-kindled,
and we exchanged those looks
of acknowledgment
too real to forget.
but seaside fantasy is born
to die in tides of reality

As the fire was burning low
and yearnings subsiding,
the earth continued its turning
and the sky cleared to reveal
a silver sliver of lunar light.
The moon that pulls people together
also sends them into flight.
but seaside fantasy is born
to die in tides of reality

Portrait of a Daughter

Exhausted at the end of another
long, lonely day of literary labor,
a sedentary odyssey over all the fallow fields
of my mind in endless efforts to find
new metaphors for old truths,
all my creative energy seemingly spent
in unproductive prodding
of an uncooperative muse,
I look up from the piles of paper,
the mess of manuscripts hiding my desk,
and by chance my glance meets the gaze
of an image of the apple of a father's eye:
eighty square inches of chemically-treated paper
capturing an otherwise lost essence of a child . . . .

> *How can it be, dear daughter,*
> *that you, a mere babe in arms*
> *not more than not so long ago,*
> *then toddler trailing pink blanket*
> *along the edge of the sea at "Folly the Beach,"*
> *and, so recently it might have been last night,*
> *a little girl with hours to curl*
> *on my lap for tales of Peter Rabbit*
> *or the venerable Mrs. Tiggy-Winkle,*
> *a lap left empty except for a now-and-then*
> *perch of the once cuddlesome kitten*
> *who in your absence grew*
> *into an inscrutable cat—*
> *how can it be that you have come so soon*
> *to the other side of childhood,*
> *a lonely country where all of us are orphaned*
> *and nursery rhymes are banned?*

How can it be that you've become
so lithe and full of life, as tall
already as your mother in memory?

How can it be that you've become
so soon such a comely teenager?
I would wager that no father in any era
has ever been ready for this marvelous
metamorphosis, this awesome transition,
this tender turning of girl-child into woman.

After a moment of mutual admiration
destined to last a lifetime,
I return refreshed to my quixotic quest,
inspired anew to pursue the composition
of poems I know so few will ever read;
but what need would I have for worldly reward
when assured of accolades of angels!

Summer Days with Daughter

The Earth tilts one way, then another.
Since the death of your mother,
the seasons slip away
faster
than I can flip my calendar.
For you to be seventeen this summer—
I simply was not ready.
To see you turn the heads of men other than me
was hard to handle.
I was startled by the someone
you had suddenly become,
bedazzled at Folly Beach
by your youthful litheness, the long reach
of your charm.
Throughout two days, two nights on the train,
you entertained me from station to station
with the music of your guitar,
your giggles,
and good-natured conversation.
In Santa Fe, the way you wore Indian earrings
enchanted me.
And going down into the Grand Canyon,
I marvelled
at how glamorous you made it look
to travel by mule.
In the capital of Utah, no Mormon
was more blue-eyed or blonder
than you.

It is October now,
our vacation days are albumed.
In this empty nest, I fill with paternal pride,
put the album aside,
and try to picture you as new co-ed
striding across the autumn-leafed campus of Cornell.
I remember well the caution
your godfather gave me years before you were born:
"Be careful what you pray for;
you may get it."

Adam's Lament

Awakening from the deepest sleep
God has ever imposed upon man,
I tried to soothe with my hand my side,
throbbing with the strangest soreness on Earth.
Then I saw you had appeared beside me.
  Awakening from the deepest sleep

The universe and you were mine.
Yours was my resolve to remain your love slave,
totally loyal, for all time.
Together, we lacked nothing we could not
have done without for another million years.
  The universe and you were mine

Those idyllic days were untimed.
A primeval eternity was in the offing.
We spent eons watching elephants
and were the world's first ornithologists.
We were intimates with all animals.
  Those idyllic days were untimed

I remained close to your unblemished belly,
content to cuddle your virginal body
until you saw one day a snake slipping through
a tight hole to strip off its old skin.
You urged me to imitate its apparent pleasure.
  I remained close to your unblemished belly

I succumbed to your sense of adventure
and thrust my uncircumcised member
through a moist orifice into a place
where no man had ever been.
You knew pain for the first time; I, a sly delight.
  I succumbed to your sense of adventure

Our post-climactic remorse was a vision of horror,
a nightmare kaleidoscope of all the horrors
of the world to come inflicted by and upon our progeny.
We previewed inquisitions, genocides,
and saw the pink horses of Hiroshima.
Our post-climactic remorse was a vision of horror

Our firstborn attributed his guilt to us,
and all suffering people pointed their fingers in blame.
Our initial instinct was to cover ourselves,
a tacit plea of guilty—yet we still maintain
the sin was not in the act, but in its shame.
Our firstborn attributed his guilt to us

The visions faded and you arose to walk away.
In the deathly stillness you voiced your only concern:
"I'm not a virgin anymore, am I?"
That was the beginning of knowledge,
the end of wisdom.
The visions faded and you arose to walk away

From behind there was the sign of the cross,
a cryptic promise in permanently creased flesh.
It rose from your toes to the tops of your buttocks,
but its bearer was not my savior—there yet was none,
For millennia to come, everyone must bear their own.
From behind there was the sign of the cross

Awakening from the deepest sleep
The universe and you were mine
Those idyllic days were untimed
I remained close to your unblemished belly
I succumbed to your sense of adventure
Our post-climactic remorse was a vision of horror
Our firstborn attributed his guilt to us
The visions faded and you arose to walk away
From behind there was the sign of the cross

Celestial Figs

*The woman was convinced. How lovely and fresh looking
it was! And it would make her so wise! So she ate some of
the fruit and gave some to her husband, and he ate it too.
And as they ate it, suddenly they became aware of their
nakedness, and were embarrassed. So they strung fig leaves
together to cover themselves around the hips.*

Genesis 3:6-7 *(The Living Bible)*

Created just a little lower than the angels,
it was only natural the first naturalists
would have an appetite for heavenly food.
And, although *no* ambrosia is complete without apples,
theirs was unique, enhanced with a handful
of purple figs we have come to call *celestial!*

But they were carried away by their taste for this
testicular treat, biting off more than two could chew.
As they feasted and frolicked beneath the fig tree,
by an epiphany they knew they were naked
and in their shame they felt constrained
to fashion organic G-strings to hide their genitals.

Forget those lies about an apple (forbidden or otherwise).
What Eve and Adam dared to eat had to grow
on the same kind of tree as the leaves they wore.
(As any nudist knows, an apple leaf
would hardly hide Eve's nonexistent navel,
much less her or Adam's pubic rise.)

Although these goings-on in the Garden
left a sour taste in the mouth of God,
it is said He not only gave His blameless son
to be the bread of life for all humanity,
but also, as tiny tokens of a nurturing love,
let us keep the sweetest figs this side of Heaven

A Touch

I ponder the contours of your body
as I would a map of Tibet—
interesting, forbidden.

> *Reference to Webster reassures us*
> *sensuality is no synonym for sin.*
> *Thus, it's fair to find Asia's*
> *earliest residents innocent*
> *in following natural instinct.*
> *The pain came only when they questioned it.*

Your pubic growth I imagine to be golden.
It remains more mysterious to me
than the Bermuda Triangle
I am allowed to enter.

> *Sixty centuries after Eden,*
> *each of us is still a leper*
> *to most of our fellow sufferers.*
> *This claim to civilization, then, is tenuous.*
> *What was healthier was lost in antiquity*
> *when our progenitors were taught not to touch.*

Do you deplore my lust?
It is innocuous;
I do not explore without license.

> *Most men have semi-sensitivity*
> *stymied by memory of medieval mores.*
> *Liberators of the spirit are cautioned*
> *to patience; told Utopia will not be built*
> > *in a day.*

You would allow access only to your lover,
unaware that he and I were making poems
on Parnassus before you were born.
We are closer than blood brothers;
he is me with another name.

It is not implied the contact people deny
would save the world, but it could inspire
a new beginning.
The lonely cannot wait forever
for a good morning kiss.
Our need demands humanity now

Route 36

to a once beautiful raccoon, nameless
but unforgettable, which I found on
this state supported animal trap—
fatally injured—whose misery I tried
to end with a tire iron
                    (June 1969)

                    I

The early morning fog lifts lazily
from western Pennsylvania,
and shrouded nature assumes
sometimes ghastly and martial shapes.

The first sun rays
rent the grey curtains,
revealing an army
of the state's most handsome denizens

lining the highway at rigid attention,
as if presenting themselves for inspection
to careless passersby,
their ringed eyes blind now
to fleeting, apathetic glances.

The sight of a dead raccoon
used to stop me.
Now,   only   my   heart   slows.

II

Like a blacksnake,
Route 36
wiggles its way
through the Keystone,

venomless
but carrying death
in 200 h.p. doses

to repel the furry inmates
imprisoned
by asphalt fences.

III

In its monotonous miles
even trees coalesce,
and we fail to see
its sole salvation:
    so many shades
    of green

—punctuated here and there
by a barnside reminder that
   Jesus Saves
or an exhortation to
      Chew
     Mail Pouch
     Tobacco

Captain Ahab's Ditty

Rub-a-dub-dub, call me Ahab,
    for I have whales on my mind
    and in my tub of a belly.
    To slay them I slip away from land
    in command of an unsinkable ship.
Rub-a-dub-dub, call me Ahab,
    for the company I would keep
    are fearsome creatures of the deep.
    They swim in the brine of my veins,
    surface in the storm behind my eyes
    (the working one as well as the egg);
    they wallow in the hollow of my leg.
Rub-a-dub-dub, call me Ahab,
    for I abhor the stability of dry land
    and love to stand and walk at odd angles.
    I have found nirvana in Neptune
    and lost nothing in Nantucket.
Rub-a-dub-dub, call me Ahab,
    or, maybe, a nautical Narcissus.
    And tell that malicious Mister Melville
    it was he who made me worship
    the salty image of the sea god
    I imagine myself to be!

In A Deserted Farmhouse

"Where have all the people gone—where and O why?"
from a folk song

A teakettle for decades
has reposed in continually deepening dust,
cold and dry,
silent as its surroundings.
A teakettle cannot sing without fire,
will not whistle without water.
Locked outside our lives
each of us is a kind of Okie
. . . sometime or another.

From the prison of an old family portrait,
the eyes of people we might have been
stare from their vacancy into ours.
A wandering tribe,
they are lost on the tundras of loneliness,
the deserts of forgotteness.
Locked outside our lives
each of us is a kind of Okie
. . . sometime or another.

Piled in a closet never fully opened
lies the clothing of childhood
of all of us who do not live
long enough to outgrow it.
Locked outside our lives

Contrition

All morality was girthed by a Bible Belt
in the rural region where I was raised
in those days before public school praises
were declared unconstitutional.
My Sunday Schooling supplemented
by the home rule of a fundamentalist father,
I inherited a rigid tradition
that took me through an Army tour, innocence intact,
while all about me buddies fell
in the war with the whores of hell as well
as other assorted enemies of the faithful.

Serving God and Caesar as chaplain's assistant,
I listened for a calling to someday fill
some Protestant pulpit.
Holiday and duty day I was purity in uniform.
Even on leave in Ireland,
having fallen for a lovely lass,
it was as a bastion of Baptist loyalty
that I declined to marry that Catholic colleen.
As a Gretna Green couple, we were not likely
to find an ecumenical bridge
over the chasm separating our pasts.

We were little more than children (of the Lord)
when we met in Dublin, and, during the next decade,
loved in absentia.
Finally, forlorn of hope of ever coming together,
we took other mates in connubial contract,
facilitating copulation free of condemnation,
public or parental.

As years pass, my marriage withers and dies,
while yours remains alive in name only.
At last, fate forces decision again.
This time we choose to lie together in disobedience
to everyone and thing except the needs of our own
prolonged loneliness—not lust, for I trust
that Christ Himself could have blest this union.
Thus, only the commandment of my earthly father
of the Old Testament is transgressed
as we undress our image-of-God bodies
of every stitch of inhibition
and celebrate total communion.

After love is made and we satisfied in sleep,
my father, who has been keeping watch from afar,
makes known his deep grief for my soul.
From beneath six feet of Carolina clay,
across six hundred or million miles of space,
he projects his grave face in agitation.
The effect is so sobering that I
in contrite consciousness sit up and cry
My associate in adultery also awakens
and, seeing me shaken, offers me a mortal solace
I may never be fully free to accept

ABOVE AND BEYOND

ABOVE AND BEYOND
heralds the headline
over the gory story
attributing posthumous glory
to this fallen instrument
                of national policy.

ABOVE AND BEYOND
describes the deeds
of this fallen son
who slew eight of the slant-eyed foe
                before he fell.

ABOVE AND BEYOND
started the story
sentimentalized by a shot
of his parents' weeping eyes.

ABOVE AND BEYOND
but without mention
of slant-eyed tears
shed for seven and one
slant-eyed sons
                of other weeping parents.

ABOVE AND BEYOND
                . . . comprehension

My Lai Meditation

My apathy has appalled my apathy
and can no longer ignore deaths
of strangers suddenly ceasing
to live in strange sounding places,
their strange-featured faces falling apart.
   My apathy has appalled my apathy

I shall take a stand and burn my soul
in a fiery poem of protest
for these who died without leaving
their names or forwarding address,
but I shall not emulate their monks.
   I shall take a stand and burn my soul

I shall canonize their anonymity,
an inadequate compensation
for persons never known, it is true.
But can I do more than pen petitions
ex post facto to purge my being
of what all of us have allowed?
   I shall canonize their anonymity

Tomorrow, I shall walk circumspectly,
stepping on no one.
I shall give my fellows the right-of-way
to seek their pleasure: a full measure
of life without fear for everyone.
   Tomorrow, I shall walk circumspectly

If God has not turned away,
I shall pray for peace,
then send a dollar to CARE
to help the injured replace
their heads, hearts, and underwear.
If God has not turned away

My apathy has appalled my apathy
I shall take a stand and burn my soul
I shall canonize their anonymity
Tomorrow, I shall walk circumspectly
If God has not turned away

For Dag Hammarskjöld

As your midnight sun began
annual hibernation
and shortening days ended
another Scandinavian summer,
faces lengthened with longer masks
of melancholy than usual.

That was September at its saddest—
                    1961.

Falling from an African sky
while flying an errand for humanity,
you have come seven thousand
final miles to a lasting peace.
It is rare,
it is the envy of a war-weary world,
it is an Uppsalan peace.

In the summer of Seventy
my nine-year pilgrimage ends
as I stand inside a cathedral,
then beside the *Hammarskjöld Familjegrav*
and resolve again to live by your *Markings*

Three for Yevgeny

(1)
You, Yevgeny Yevtushenko, proclaim
            my country's flag stars
                        bullet holes

but what do you name
      the hammer and sickle
      that nails individuals' hopes
      and cuts helpless nations' throats
on a field of red

                        red
                        red
                  rape red
                        red
                  rape red
                        bled
                        bled
                              from free hearts

(2)
Nineteen centuries ago
your hammer and sickle
would have been used
to drive the nails
and wound His side

(3)
Times change;
      now you call
            your czars
                  by other names

War Games

Beard and passivity belie my past:
In the Cold War
of the almost forgotten Fifties,
I was a soldier for NATO,
one of many in West Germany
always alert to the threat
of Soviet aggression.

Officially declared combat ready
by Pentagon peace makers/breakers,
my battle group was seasoned
by ceaseless training
over countless miles of Bavarian terrain
and a sprinkling of experience
from hotter wars.

We knew strategic possibilities
of places tourists never view
and were vigilant
through all kinds of rotten weather,
but we never got to glimpse
a Russian.

Out of step, now, with military movements,
I shuffle my feet, let my hair lengthen,
and grow philosophical about the people
we were ready to kill.

I stroke my beard
and shake my shaggy head
at the dreaded thought of that M-1,
which hung so patriotically
from my shoulder,
spiralling a slug through heart or brain
of one of my strange-named counterparts:

Would a Geneva Convention
have found me as guilty
of crime as Cain?
And what if such an enemy had been named
by birth-proud parents *Yevgeny*

Cairo—February 12, 1970

Ovens of the Third Reich have cooled,
their stokers interred
or forced into hiding forever.
A few have been reduced to dust.
And who would question the righteousness
of such retribution?
Still, it is no final solution
to the shortcomings of man,
and the tradition they kindled
continues to glow
as a bold new generation of Jews
takes its own turn at baking bodies.
But these somber sons of Moses are militant,
modern, loathe to fiddle with slow-burning ovens
when bombs can do the job
seventy times faster.
They re-cross a blood-named sea
once opened for their ancestors
going the other way.
They strike like phantoms
to shatter again the Delta's calm.
Struggle-fatigued judgment selects an unlikely target.
Stunned eyes of school children stare skyward
for the split second before the searing burst
of napalmic sun turns morning into heliocentric noon.
Teeth, too, are lost to implement the ancient dictum

Eye for eye, tooth for tooth,
hand for hand, foot for foot,
Burning for burning,
wound for wound . . . .

Vengeance is wrought,
        a minaret teeters,
                mothers wail in Arabic . . . .
No, these sounds are of no living language:
they are as old as the forked tongue named hate

The Fort Jackson Bugles

In all my life
I have never had a desire
to be an early riser.
Three years of military duty
merely convinced me
that getting up early is for the birds;
that reveille is for those roosters
who believe in bugles,
a queer breed of bird
which crows a loud complaint
even on the day of reenlistment.

I fly with another flock
and a decade after discharge
continue to cringe at abrupt awakenings
before daybreak.
The bugles blown at ancient Jericho
couldn't have been more disconcerting
than those that still reverberate
in my memory of Fort Jackson, South Carolina.

Often an hour before dawn
they heralded the olive drab day,
tearing down the walls of G. I. minds
to re-make them into warriors:
Gentile and Jewish alike,
black as well as white.
The Fort Jackson bugles
discriminated equally against everyone.

The people of Munich pleaded ignorance
to the doings in nearby Dachau.
I wonder if the citizens of Columbia
ever hear the Fort Jackson bugles

Exile

My Charleston childhood was interrupted
nightly by sounds of ship horns
passing the Battery in briny East Bay.
I heard these and dreamed of someday
sailing through the seven seas,
finding then leaving proverbial loves
                    in all salty ports.
But these dreams were never launched;
my travels were never so romantic.

When I attained the age of idealism
years later, I began to dream again,
but of something dearer, an America
with its people nearer each other
than ever before.
To see if this were possible,
I did my own rambling sample survey
in Santa Fe and Seattle,
in Nashville and New York,
in Winston-Salem and western Pennsylvania.

I found the potential promising,
the process exhausting.
Fatigued, I deserted the issues
to seek my solace in a return home
                    and to romance.

Now, my distances are measured
in ties that bind railroad lines—
so many to a mile,
so many to a reverie—
the count coming back greater always
than that on the outbound track.

Upon arrival I find everything
the same in my dear old hometown:
few structures going upwards;
preservation societies not letting any go down.
Slaves still come and go,
enjoying the probation
given them ten decades ago.
News is still of the war,
the one we were lucky to lose,
but would have won if our great-grands
hadn't tired themselves out whuppin' the foe.

At last I recognize Thomas Wolfe
and I have been traveling
in the same compartment—years apart.
He has taught my kind a lesson
I have learned the hard way

Hampton Park Revisited

(for my mother)

Time has taken me far
from these green lawns and duck ponds;
it is the same time
that takes us from each other.
But you and I return this morning
to impede its passing a bit,
and sit on a hospitable bench
to saturate ourselves
with the sun of early autumn.

In this position of rest we are free
to re-live a favorite memory:
a child of Sunday dressed in white,
romping over all the places of play in sight,
while you watch without scolding
for the grass-stained sailor suit pants
you will have to scrub so long on Monday.

A war was raging then,
far beyond the Battery
in battles I'd have to study later.
Those were the years of half-moon headlights
and funny little stamps you had to trade
for shoes and sugar,
although the sweetness of your smile
was never rationed.

Today, different wars are waged—
or maybe they're the same
with only names changed
to protect the wagers.
Still, this arsenal city's
peace of place and place of peace
have remained intact.

Thirty years have passed
since you last brought me to play in this park.
Now, with matured muscles
and a sister's assistance,
I try to return the favor
by guiding you slowly over the same paths
where once you watched me run.

Time has taken me far
from these green lawns and duck ponds;
it is the same time
that takes us from each other

Sometimes Boys Can See Further

(for Jamie)

"Sometimes I feel so happy it makes tears in my eyes.
Then I can see rainbows in my tears."   —Jamie Smith
                                                              Age 4

For seven months
you spelunkered
in a prenatal cave
too narrow to contain
your curiosity.

When the groundhog instinct
grew too great
to let you rest,
you climbed from the cave
headfirst,
and, seeing no shadow,
were convinced
that winter should end.

Although your spirit was strong
and willing to venture
further than any umbilical cord
can stretch,
your flesh was too weak
to survive
without the treatment
which scarred your eyes.

We may never understand
why the cost of this salvation
was weakened sight,
although it delights me to learn
your vision was not impaired

Eugene Argues With Reason After Meeting Grace

There was a meeting of eyes,
I only know what mine saw.
a coupling of hands,
A moment longer than courtesy required.
a vague promise:
"We'll see each other again."
Words mean to me what they say.
Nothing more.
It was a moment of truth
I wanted to be the moment of Grace.
I shall term it graceful anyhow.
What's with all these words?
Words mean to me what they say,
and it was not the first time
I fell infatuated with an image.
You poets are as naive as Pavlov's pups.
Yes, we're conditioned
to respond to such stimuli.
My eyes drool for her.
Fool, she was flattered, amused, amazed,
admitting beauty only in brown shadows
which light half her face.
To respond to such stimuli,
to bask in the warmth of her shadows,
I would defy convention.
Yes, I would dare to defy you.
Your sense of beauty
is as warped as your wit.
Can't you see that beauty is more
than summation of facial features?
It's something beyond.
Pig, I leave you to wallow . . . .
in the trough of sweet fantasy?

Remembering the Girl at the Party

Chicly bared,
her navel
stared
at me
like
a third eye,
while fourth and fifth
peaked
between the weave
straining to restrain them.

In the middle
of my head,
a convoluted eye
continues
to stare back

To the Girl Who Misguided Me in Halifax

To most of us in the U.S.
your Maritime Provinces seem as inaccessible
as the seat of your affection was to me.
From nearly every place we dwell,
a trip to the outer edge of the northeast
is simply too far to travel
for a strawberry smile
or a strawberry parfait
or any other Nova Scotian serendipity.

Except for the explorer instinct in me
—or maybe it was the romantic strain—
I, too, might not have taken that train
from Montreal on the long haul eastward
through Quebec and New Brunswick
to the very heart of Halifax.
But, then, I was glad I had,
if only for the long, coveside embrace
that ended the day you gave
to show me why you're a Haligonian.

Only after a cowardly delay
did the poverty of your soul reveal itself,
and I must declare you gave me something
no customs agent would care about,
your embrace an empty gesture.

Back, now, in Appalachian isolation
with a woman I have loved longer,
I ponder the chance that paired us
on the periphery of a new world.

I know we will never meet by choice

The Last Tryst

Into my heart's treasury
I slipped a coin . . . .
—Sara Teasdale

(Our weekly passion spent, we fall apart on sheets
illicitly stained before us by legions of lovers like us,
and savor mirrored forms lying side by side overhead.
Beside the bed a digital clock signals, then,
the end of another hour of stolen bliss—and I plea:)
    Let's quickly kiss—
    and let this risky tryst be our last.

It may sound like cliche, but must be said—
we really can't go on meeting like this.
These titillating times together are fraught
with potential for pain, embarrassment.
If ever caught here, how could we explain?
    Let's quickly kiss—
    and let this risky tryst be our last.

For Christ's sake, let's quit while we're ahead,
forsake our sweet Thursdays bed,
and from now on lie in lust only with—yes,
the trusting spouses whose surnames we share.
In your heart, you know we couldn't bear to hurt them.
    Let's, quickly kiss—
    and let this risky tryst be our last.

Just as we have loved and comforted each other,
let us dwell on the needs of the unknowing
innocent who love us as well, honor our vows,
accept the constraints of prior commitments,
seek solace in the calmer comforts of home.
    Let's quickly kiss—
    and let this risky tryst be our last.

The roulette wheel of romance keeps on spinning,
but it's naive to assume we'll go on winning.
By ceasing this cheating now and beating the odds,
we can keep in our hearts' treasuries what we've won,
precious coins, currency for fantasy for years to come.
   Let's quickly kiss—
   and let this risky tryst be our last.

Passion and Ice

All tasteless attempts at wit
notwithstanding,
my malice toward your marriage
is not unmitigated.
A wholesome side of my lonesome psyche
wishes you happiness at the hearth,
long life
with him who held your hand
through sorrows
until he won your heart
(not to mention the prize of your thighs,
the comfort of pillow-soft breasts,
and, for blissful rest,
the support of firm buttocks).
May your bonding be for better, not worse;
for richer, not poorer.
In sickness and in health let it be steadfast
in withstanding
the side effects of familiarity.

The darker side of me will disagree:
This hypocritical half would sooner see you widow—
young, lithe, elegant in black,
receptive to its shallow sympathy,
consoled, ready to be made merry,
ready to rendezvous on a Carolina dune
we left so long ago too soon,
ready to seek in the failing light
of The Fall
whatever apples may be salvaged
for a precarious season
of passion and ice.

Daily,
I reject this reverie.
Hour by hour
I wrestle with its wickedness:

O Lord, I pray,
please take her image away
and let my aching cease.
Allow me passion, but grant it
with Thy salving peace.
Satisfy me with surrogates
of Thy choice before it is too late.
And deny me my voice
when I would curse my fate.
Soften my heart for the cuckold.
Harden my need for someone new.

Disquiet

Like deceptively gentle raindrops
which wear away mountains
over eons,
too many seasons of contentment
have eroded your resolve, your troth,
have slowly readied you to see the truth:
This is the disquiet
you covet
after endless days of domestic tranquility,
countless nights of connubial bliss,
a quartet of kids
clamoring for candied apples or goodnight kiss,
a dark-featured spouse all of you call "Father"
(a John Doe jealous of his rights),
a cedar-shingled house beside the sea,
filled with the familial and mortgage-free.
This is a watershed between basic needs:
the comfort of the familiar/
the novelty of the new,
a reminder of something almost forgotten,
but too good to lose and so much older
you are startled to find it again in the kindly
face and firmer body of a bolder stranger.
This balance is as beautiful as it is precarious:
Tip it either way
and
you may never be the same

Menu for a Poet's Breakfast

(for Morning)

Sunshine and Orange Musejuice
      (from the South)
Filet of Tenderloin
      (leftover from last night,
      but still tender and strong
      enough to support a sunny-side up)
Fruit of a Fowl
      (As You Like It)
Butter-Basted Toast
      (covered with a sonnet of
      lingonberries from Sweden—
      chew iambically)
Stimulating Coffee
      (made with beans from Brazil
      or Colombia, freshly ground—
      try sipping it in dactylics)
Sugar, Salt, Pepper, and Inspiration
      (for a Morning poem)

---

*This breakfast is on the house.
Have a nice life!*

Paean to a Girl In a Poetry Workshop

You remind me of a cathedral
I could fill to legal capacity
as a congregation of one.

You attract me to hours of worship
from across a wilderness the width
of a wide table, a reality
I am able to cross only under
cover of metaphor or daydreams at night.
The rites of such an existential faith
are not a part of our weekly meetings.

When I transcend the desert between us,
I stand transfixed before the twin-towered
splendor of pointed arches
soaring skyward with purpose:
to direct the eyes of men toward angels.

I knock at doors some know as Heaven's gates
and tremble till the priest in you
appears with the open arms of invitation.

We confess together and as one
consecrate the elements of communion.
To take this body and blood I lay my own
the length of your nave—*Kyrie eleison.*

This is still a daydream
which brings the blessing
of being in you no closer.
My metaphors remain metaphors.

Incidentally, I like your poetry.

A Poet Learns The New Math

I come home with a body
tired from two days travel,
a mind wearied by too many weeks' work
as a poet-in-the-schools.
I come home with my love for you
  ivided
  d

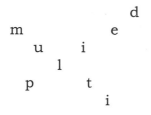

intensified
by the absence—
and something approaching adoration
for your letting me learn
to love another
briefly, but beautifully

Poet in Trees

HELP! I'm in a real piccadilly
seventeen floors over New York City,
and though never before a believer
in astral projection find my body
suddenly soulless as that eternal
part of me seeks that sweeter,
ethereal essence of you.
But poets must be allowed to live in trees—
even artificial, soul-sucking ones like these—
to seek their muse; it's the only way
they can be of use to others and themselves.
So, if you think my poetic perch too precarious,
consider its Southern exposure and what
this means to me: "It's finger lickin' good."
Don't shout if I seem to be too far out,
and please do not disrupt my repose,
for poetry grows often in odd places
and even some of my own finest lines
have sprouted on limbs.
Remember that we, too, have sailed
beyond the horizon of permissible love
and upon my return to earth will live
again in New Heights of Erotica, Pennsylvania.
Then I shall confess an affair
with a French-American lady in New York harbor
who has been giving peace for years.
(But I did not mount her; it was only an act
                        of circumnavigation.)

Carolina Catechism

My dear departed father,
forever fundamentalist,
was as stern as his namesake,
the Apostle Paul.

Indeed, he believed in the banana
as the cause of Eve and Adam's fall
after they ate an apple
more aphrodisiac than allegory.

A prodigal son for loving
poetry more than prophecy,
I honor the holy but
believe in both metaphorically

Overdose

For years I was a thief,
stealing apples
from the tree of time
to support a habit
not sanctioned by society-by-large.

Drugged
by a daily dose of words
injected directly into my lifestream,
a nagging muse
on my back,
and with the law and order
of middle age closing in,

I decided
to make my break,
to take leave from all other pursuits
in order to poet full time.

I found life as a free-lance fugitive
painful,
and burning sensations
having nothing to do with inspiration
troubled my chest.

When my concern
turned more to cholesterol and coronaries
than creativity,
I became frightened and complained
to colleagues who had elected to remain
behind the bars of tenure, security,
content (or resigned)
to administer to their own addictions
only after midnight, weekends,
whenever time could be purloined.

Those familiar with the symptoms
were sympathetic;
but, they said, it was my head
and not my heart that needed examining

At the Writers Conference

Here we are: high
in the Green Mountains of Vermont,
far from Arkansas and Ohio;
here we are: high with expectations
of what we might do, of what we might write,
of what great we might emulate.
Here we are: far
from the restraints of hearth.
We come
unencumbered by children,
unburdened by husbands, unweighed by wives.
We come
without obligation to observe convention.
We come
to be novel,
to play like playwrights.
We come
licensed to be poetic.
We come
to float like untethered balloons,
and for a dozen days
we can be the free spirits we write about,
which is to say, we can be what we envy
most of the seasons of our lives.
We may even know someone new,
learning in the fling something useful,
if not about writing, at least about love.
And with luck we will get a glimpse
of ourselves before we return to realities:
relationships and responsibilities
left simmering on back burners
back at home

For John Berryman

Lying beside the Grand Canal
at Baggot Street Bridge,
Patrick Kavanagh discovered
the comfort of not caring,
the solace in laughing
at one's self.
Had you really known him
when you did the Henry thing in Dublin,
Paddy could have taught you
his potent antidote
for the fatal boredom
of taking one's life
too seriously.

John, did you find this joy,
finally,
at the bottom
of some other bridge?
In the terrible quiet,
your muted answer
asks other questions

Lines for a Young Poet

Poets should sleep sometimes
with the similes
and metaphors of their fantasies.
You have learned this early,
and that's not bad.
If I had it to do again,
I, too, would seek emancipation early.

Your poems have feeling,
your work a central nervous system.
Its hint in your smile
may lead many
to seek solace within your words.
I pray you will never
betray our trust.

You have dark hair like a Hellene,
and that reminds me of the Greeks
who called poets makers.
Your creation is classic.
You make lines of love

Rather Than Olives

It may be true
that Adam and Eve started
this whole screwing match,
but to place on their naked shoulders
the entire burden is unfair.

Noah and his crew
must share the blame
for our present predicament.
They knew what could happen,
yet failed to form in the ark
what would have been the world's first
planned parenthood association,

ignoring the example
of their content-to-be-continent
animals,
and choosing at the critical moment
to eat the dove
rather than olives

Haiku for the Happily Married

To be happily
married means never having
to say you're horny.

Haiku of a Whale

Call me Moby Dick,
for I have swallowed the great
white shark, *Jaws* and all.

Ahead of the Game

You're so virile and chief of state,
ruling over a kingdom vast and great.
What's a poor girl to do,
losing her head over you—
you're Henry number eight!

Irish Mist

After he left Dublin,
she went to confession,
said a dozen rosaries,
and cried five days.
No wonder
devout Ireland's
so damp

Californication

They have come.   They come.   They keep coming.
They arrive in singles and flocks from all ethnic stocks
and every other state of good and evil,
Biblically innumerable (seven times seven).
They come to this state of mind slightly higher
west of the Rockies, far, far west of Easternism.

One Pittsburgh miner has come for the finer
particled smog of Los Angeles;
a Texan ashamed of assassination
also seeks solace in the city of angels,
but avoids the Ambassador Hotel.

Conservative John B.s from all over come fleeing
the spread of creeping Communism.
Monogamists come to double their holdings,
the clothed to strip, the naked to dress themselves in sunshine.
The lonely are here to share their longings.

In general, the hung up have come out to shake loose,
to let it all hang out, to live it up,
to live and live faster because there's more life here
than they've ever seen before, more life to live here
in twenty-four hours than in any Ohio lifetime,
and more quasi-lives flushed into the Pacific every day
than born annually in New Hampshire.

Still they come. They come ever faster to this magnet of
minds running like a chicken with its wishbone plucked of luck.
They come dragging to a drugged culture loved by some
who predict their abode will become America's Atlantis,
as well as by others who hate all off-beat lovers.
Thus hated and loved by all kinds of everyone,
the most popular operation has become the Caesarian
so pleasure will never be stretched out of shape
for any and all californicating comers

Moment

Like two young gulls
from different flocks,
flying solo and afraid
to adventure too far
over uncharted seas,
the trajectories of our lives
met only once,
were parallel
in a narrow moment of sunlight
before diverging
to opposite infinities

Nomad

All my life I have been a nomad
on northern deserts of loneliness—
not by choice, but by design
of something I cannot control.

There was a time
when oases were frequent.
Humping along on the camel of youth,
I happened upon them without effort.

Once I laid claim to a uniquely
beautiful one as my very own,
was as attentive to it
as a nomadic way of life allows.

But the need to wander took me away often,
and during the absence of one such odyssey
a brighter-than-usual sun
left my oasis changed, uninhabitable.

The sands seem endless now
and shift in new directions.
The carcass of my camel lies buried
in some barren place I know
I shall never find again

Living at the Edge

For days on end
I run beneath the surface
of my emotions
like a World War Two submarine
on lonely patrol beneath the sea,
needing to come up sometimes
to recharge the batteries,
needing to come up,
      needing . . .
           needing

Going for the Gold Bug

Forsaking files, phones, paper clips,
reports no one will ever read with relish
but which I Labor over and write every week
in order to pay my rent,
I gather the remnants of my wits
and leave the summer-steamy city
at the end of almost every sticky day,
crossing intersections, bridges, causeway,
a routine geared to remove myself
from prosaic present into vestiges
of a more Poetic past.

Beyond the far side of the harbor
and on the other side of the haze,
I reach the solace of Sullivan's Island
and on the beach below its lighthouse
abandon automobile, wristwatch, responsibility.
I find my favorite secluded dune facing west
for watching weary suns settle low
over Charleston's steeples and roofs,
then open a notebook ever ready to record
the most poignant poem ever written.

I wait to write until I feel moonlight fall
on the Houses of Usher, Rutledge, and all the rest.
Again I hesitate, for it is too early
for recognition and, for fortune, too late.
I curse my fate, uncork a flask
of sour mash inspiration,
imagine myself successor to Edgar Allan Poe

Psyching Out My Psychiatrist

"I have," my psychiatrist says, "these sinister images
    hovering in my head:
a wife, with insufficient reason, leaving me,
    another lying dead."
Thus begins one of our typical sessions face-to-face,
and I decide it's time for me to get on *his* case.
I reply, "I advise you to try poetry as therapy.
It can help you sort the sordid from the sweet, help you see
what is and what is not your responsibility.
Believe me—if I, an honest poet, have any credibility—
you must accept the fact that each mate
    made her own decision.
Blaming yourself for their tragic choices
    is needless, destructive self-derision.
What you should do in fifty lines or fewer
    (and unrhymed are best)
is to exorcise their ghosts, put them finally to rest.
Meanwhile, do not doubt your manhood
    or think yourself any less.
Many sensitive men survive on the edge of madness—
thrive there and create. We can see it with Mozart and Swift:
Amadeus made immortal music;
    biting satire was the Good Dean's gift."
Then, having been compassionate and truthful,
I allow my psychiatrist a chance to be useful:
"And how about my own writing," I ask, "what do you think?
I need your help—you're the shrink.
Every night I should be home working in my study,
but—what do I do?
Well, I'm usually out womanizing or drinking with a buddy.
Nights with my typewriter are few."

"Don't worry," he consoles me, "your inspiration
    is The Three E's:
the emotions, encounters, experiences of life,
    things of birds and bees.
Such lines you won't find sitting alone
    looking into your navel.
They're lyrics of real life, waiting beside your father's
    grave, in a lover's arms, or in wine at candlelit table.
So, go out and find yourself—have some fun, some grief,
    any kind of caper.
And stop wasting your time with shrinks—
    do your emoting on paper."

As our fifty-minute hour of mutual psychomassage
    comes to an end,
we have a heightened awareness of friend helping friend.
And, seeing our respective psychoses resolved,
    gone with hardly a trace,
we dry our eyes, rise, and embrace.

Ashley River

In the beginning a spring bubbles up
from a humble hole in the fertile earth
of Lowcountry South Carolina,
somewhere due west of Summerville
in a woodsy corner of Dorchester County
not far from the farm on which my father was born.

From this sparsely-peopled place—nowhere near
as renown as the city at the tip of which
the Ashley combines with Cooper counterpart
to impart an Atlantic Ocean—it, with a trickle
of a start, in a mere thirty miles,
more or less, grows to a kind of greatness,
stirs the hearts of thousands, creates
proportionately more nostalgia
than the Nile, as much as the Mississippi.

Unpretentiously, it passes plantations,
wanders through woods, laps the edges
of gardens famous throughout the world.
It courses between banks benignly shaded
by ancient oaks, tall pines, and magnolias
more fragrant than metaphors can convey.
Under these trees one sees randomly discarded
symbols of civilization: condoms, oyster shells,
Firestones, the rusty frame of a boy's bicycle.

Downstream the river's marshy shoulders are
a home for herons, egrets, and other waders.
Here twice it's bridged but not abridged, serves
as a moat on one side of The Citadel, a boundary
for the wet side of Brittlebank Park,
a backdrop for baseball played before dark.
Farther into the city, it is scenery
for the sick in several hospitals,
the elderly stacked in condominiums,
Coast Guardsmen weary from being *Semper Paratus.*

At the Battery, it waxes elegant,
provides a setting for sailing into the sunset,
a rippling background for pubescent passion,
a place to feel pride in one's communal past,
an atmosphere to be nearer one's maker.

Becoming part of Charleston Harbor,
it is a cornucopian source of seafood
and solace for all the city's citizens
regardless of the color of their blood,
the natives as well as the naturalized.

All along the way the river's royal name
has been used to christen Carolina children.
Beyond the jetties and continental shelf,
the Ashley's issue is too cosmopolitan
to be considered ours alone

Praise God for Grits

And why not when we are blessed
with those extra moments
of a Saturday morning
to sit and savor
a breakfast of something more
than cold milk and cereal?

Bowing now over these tiny bits of corn
a foot from my face,
I, far from ancestral home,
far from the rural region
where I was reared on grits
and fear of God,
far away from the familiar,
far away and far out
on the periphery of life itself
for a far too long time,
thank Him for this heap
of hot, pure white, mouth-watering goodness,
spiced by salt of His earth and peaked
by butter the color of sunlight
pouring into my bachelor abode
and into my newly salvaged psyche.

I thank Him for being there at the end
of a year I almost ended early;
I thank Him for making me want to wait
for a different kind of destiny;
I thank Him for a heart
that, having bled, still beats;
for blond hair that never thins
and continues to lengthen;
for a penis that did not atrophy—
and promise of purer places to put it.

I thank Him for victory over vindictiveness:
for being able to forgive
and almost able to forget
the insensitive iniquity of a former spouse
afflicted even yet with v. d. of the personality.

I thank Him for a few new friends,
and old friends refound
(among whom may be a long-lost muse);
I thank Him for poems from years past
written well enough to last,
and for the possibility of more to come.

Again, I thank Him for these grits,
for these great little bits of wholesomeness,
so nicely flavored by all the good things
they go with,
for these grits, which, though vitaminless,
nourish Southern souls nonetheless.

> *Praise God from whom all blessings flow.*
> *Praise Him, all creatures here below.*
> *Praise Him above, ye heavenly hosts.*
> *Praise Father, Son and Holy Ghost.*

Praise God for grits.
Amen.

The Eagle Within

Wanting to emulate the eagle
which is inside each of us,
to forget for an hour
the cares of the terrestrial,
I enter the womb of a sailplane
to be reborne aloft,
leave the element of my species,
rise above the restraints
                of the wingless,
come home to the spirit
which soars within me

Sailplane Pilot's Fantasy in Flight

Soaring in the reverie
      of pure and silent flight,
motorless and more than a mile above
      the level of the sea,
my highly seasoned sense of sight
      is startled by a smile of love
on a cloudface as beatific
      as the visage of Beatrice
seen by a dumfounded, grounded Dante
      someplace no more pacific
and yet no less ephemeral than this.
      Tonight it shall surely haunt me:
The memory of lips, nose, chin—
      sculptured features as soft
as her cumulus cotton candy coiffure—
      in an essence too thin
to exist anywhere but thermally aloft,
      far from dirt and din, heaven-secure.

Sign Language

After years of self-seeking exile
while hungering for home,
and a long day's drive down I-95,
I see up ahead the sign:

**SOUTH CAROLINA
STATE LINE**

I make another sign
as I drive across,
touching fingers to forehead and
heart.

For me it is still
a religious experience,
the teachings of Thomas Wolfe
notwithstanding

Celestial Navigation

*

This had to be the star that Zoroaster saw
in his mind a half-millennium earlier;
this had to be the long-awaited star for naught
in nighttime Persian skies was ever pearlier.

*

All the magi were delighted indeed to see
this heavenly sign, knowing what our prophet said,
and all of us agreed to choose by lot and send
a few of us with gifts to whomever it led.

*

In ensuing centuries we became well known.
And while there are those who forever call us wise,
we were only aware of all we did not know
and able to give treasures money never buys.

*

In search of a source of new, enlightened wisdom,
wherever that star led, we were willing to go.
We humped across countless dunes as undulating
as endless waves and over mountains capped with snow.

*

Our nocturnal pace slowed for nothing, our camels
so content, those surefooted ships of the desert
who bore with dromedary dignity their loads
of men and food enough to keep them fit, alert.

The camels carried, too, a cargo of caskets
carefully filled with frankincense and myrrh and gold:
fitting gifts for a new king destined to die young,
according to what the prophet Micah foretold.

*

For a fortnight we followed until finally
the star stood still above a town we thought too small
to be the birthplace of royalty, but as we
entered a stinking stable we knew, regardless

*

of the circumstances of such a humble birth,
we stood before a babe unique in all the earth.

Love After the Flood

(for my Mary)

Amid the floodlike debris of divorce,
the delirium which follows destruction
of the only world one has known, long I lay
exhausted with sodden spirit, wondering
why the Lord of hosts, allegedly omnipresent,
was nowhere near when I needed Him most.

At last at a rising of the sun,
I recalled His compassion for the crew
of the ark, who in surviving the Flood
feared another, and considered His colorful
promise to spare their descendants
from such a painful fate ever again.

In a wretched state of weakened faith
and needy flesh, seeking more than reminder
of ancient lore, I asked for a sign
for myself and fell asleep, dreaming then
of a rainbow seeming to arch over
an answer, a form too far away to identify.

Awakening, I abided the actualization
of that sweet dream, watching the sun
routinely rise and set a thousand times
while waiting to see whose face
would come into focus, waiting while
its bearer grew from beauty to beauty.

Today, far away from those flood plains
of past adversity, I disembark from the ark.
My odyssey is over. I have come home
to find the face is yours and you,
like Noah's returning dove, promising love.
Redeemed, I relish the irony of your being:

Namesake of the Mother of God.

Joy/*La Joie*

(at home, Charleston)

The feelings that flow between us when
we make love in the night, then fall asleep,
reflect, like Carolina sunlight reflects
from the shiny hardwood floors of our bedroom,
as expressions of joy in the morning—
except, of course, when suppressed by workaday stress.

(on vacation, Québec)

Without crossing ocean we come to new continent,
traveling a thousand miles of tiring highway
to visit a city a century older than our own.
Here, where we feel so free to be walled in,
so light in the clear and cooler Canadian air,
so *joyeux* just to be together all day for a change
and not only, as at home, all night,
this long-awaited vacation coincides,
courtesy of fate, with Québec's Summer Festival.
Amidst musicians, jugglers, and others making
these days idyllic for many, in lingering twilight
we take walks on Dufferin Terrace, as high over
the St. Lawrence as we are on each other.
At the Auberge du Tresor we sleep late
and celebrate with endless French-Canadian kisses,
wondering how to declare to customs the priceless
worth of take-home memories for which there is no form.

The long drive home is shortened by conversation
touching everything from vacation to years-ago wedding,
but such is not ceaseless, and poignant pauses
let us listen again and again to our favorite movement
from the *Royal Fireworks Music*, music for the moment
we turned from the altar and faced the world as one:
"La Réjouissance"

My Solemn Vow

In the name of God, I, [Eugene], take you, [Mary],
to be my wife, to have and to hold from this day
forward, for better for worse, for richer for poorer,
in sickness and in health, to love and to cherish,
until we are parted by death. This is my solemn vow.
          —The Book of Common Prayer

At night I am your angel.
Lightly I sleep near you
or stay awake to hear you in case
this chemotherapy-induced distress
rises to the level of audible pain.
Alas, as steadfast as St. George,
I would have slain for you
an evil fire-breathing dragon
with the lance of my love
or, barehanded, battled any other fierce beast.
At least such an enemy is visible
and easier to vanquish.
Conversely, against cancer, those minute
bits of malignancy which multiply like mice—
and against the poison used to poison them,
I often fluster, feel frustrated, impotent.
Even so, I know I cannot acquiesce
to such an anomaly of nature.
In a perfect place no one as kindhearted as you
would ever have to face the heartbreaking loss
of even half of her signature breasts
or single strand of crowning-glory hair
to something so fearsome.
As statistics confirm, however, our universe,
if not getting worse, still has far to go
before the fair sex get a fair shake from fate.

Therefore, taking a worthy cue from you
and confronting the challenge of cancer,
    I resolve not to relent,
        never to surrender,
            to keep the faith,
                to honor my vow.

At night I am your angel:
I cry silently,   love loudly,   pray unceasingly.

The Poet's Notes

1. The absence of a period at the end of most of these poems reflects the notion, whimsical perhaps, that a poem does not have to end with a period, but can continue forever.

2. "Folly Beach Hotdogs" was composed at the beach in May 1968, the day after my father's funeral. Now, as then, "I still come to the beach" for hotdogs and solace.

3. "Edisto Hours" is dedicated to Amy and Allen, whose description of a reconciliatory weekend inspired this poem. "Praise God for Grits" is also dedicated to Allen.

4. "Preservation Society" is a literary response to *View of Mulberry Plantation*, a painting by Thomas Coram in the Gibbes Museum of Art in Charleston.

5. "Carolina Sands" was the first of five of these poems brilliantly choreographed and performed by Charleston's Robert Ivey Ballet. The others are "Perennial," "Moment," "Celestial Navigation," and "Summer Days with Daughter." The music used for the latter was the "Spring" movement from *Three Botticelli Pictures* by Respighi.

6. "Carolina Sands" and "Carolina Sands II" are dedicated to Britt, a long-ago love. In the latter poem is a reference to Dafydd ab Gwilym, a 14th Century Welsh poet said to have sent love poems to his girlfriend Morfudd via sea gulls.

7. "A Long Way from New Orleans" and "At Trinity College" have references to J. P. Donleavy's novel *The Ginger Man*.

8. For a key image in "Perennial," I thank Phyllis, who wrote to me once, " . . . you will taste the sea in me." The poems "Carolina Rose," "Passion and Ice," and "Lines for a Young Poet" are dedicated to her.

9. "Adam's Lament" and "My Lai Meditation" employ a stanzaic technique I first saw in James Dickey's poem "On the Hill Below the Lighthouse." "Summer Swimmer" employs a variation on this technique, beginning (rather than ending) with a gathering of the refrain lines from each stanza.

10. The italicized lines in "After Inniskeen" appear on a plaque on a small cross over Patrick Kavanagh's grave at Inniskeen, County Monaghan, Ireland. My most delightful literary discovery during an academic year at Trinity College (1969-1970) was Kavanagh's eminently accessible poetry. A Trinity professor, poet Brendan Kennelly, led me to this discovery, for which this poem is dedicated to him.

11. "To A New Son," "The Words," and "Metaphors Be With You" were inspired by and are dedicated to my son Paul. His image, incidentally, graces the cover of *South Carolina State Line*.

12. New Mexico is called the "Land of Enchantment." The poem title "In the Land of Disenchantment" is a play on that.

13. Near the end of "Transition" the Greek author referred to is Nikos Kazantzakis.

14. Parts of a traditional bedtime prayer were used in "Prayer." During childhood I recited nightly:
> *Now I lay me down to sleep.*
> *I pray the Lord my soul to keep.*
> *If I should die before I wake,*
> *I pray the Lord my soul to take.*

—usually adding something like "And God bless mama and daddy, and Skibo (my dog) and Bubba (my brother)."

15. Since the first in 1968, lung transplant surgery has become so commonplace as to be no longer newsworthy.

16. The photograph described in "Portrait of a Daughter" ("eighty square inches . . .") was used for the cover of this book. I took this photo of my daughter Troye in the summer of 1981, when she was 12, at the annual wild pony swim in Chincoteague, Virginia. The photo seems to convey the essence of a girl child's transition to womanhood. It's always been one of my favorite images of Troye, who remains the apple of my eye.

17. Although "Summer Days with Daughter" was written five years after the cover photo was taken, the two seem to complement each other perfectly.

18. In "Adam's Lament" (previously titled "An Original Sin") "the pink horses of Hiroshima" is an image inspired by John Hersey's description, in his 1946 book *Hiroshima*, of horses whose hides had been burned off by the atomic blast.

19. More dedications: "In A Deserted Farmhouse" to Don Wilson. "ABOVE AND BEYOND" to former U.S. Senator Eugene McCarthy, an early critic of our country's misguided war in Viet Nam. "My Lai Meditation" to Richard Ryan. "War Games" to the late Vernon Ward, who as editor of *Tar River Poets* (now *Tar River Poetry*) honored me as the featured poet of *TRP* several issues after William Stafford had been similarly featured.

20. The italicized lines in "Cairo—February 12, 1970" are from Exodus 21:24-25.

21. More dedications: "Grandfather" to V.V. "First Wife" to
C.K. "Disquiet" to Karen. "Menu for a Poet's Breakfast" to
Troye and Paul's grandmother, affectionately called
"Morning." "Haiku of a Whale" to Ed Grejda, an authority on
the works of Herman Melville. "Californication" to Tom Kiley.
"Moment" to Pat. "The Last Tryst" to Ann.

22. The setting for Poe's well-known story "The Gold Bug" is
Sullivan's Island.

23. "Psyching Out My Psychiatrist" is dedicated to Bob, a
dear, eminently insightful friend. No one has encouraged me
more as a poet.

24. "Ashley River"—*Semper Paratus* ("Always Ready") is the
motto of the U.S. Coast Guard.

25. "Celestial Navigation"—Some Biblical scholars hold that
the Three Wise Men, or Magi, mentioned in the Gospel of
Matthew were, in fact, Zoroastrian priests. (See, for example,
Paul William Roberts' fascinating 1995 book *In Search of the
Birth of Jesus*.) The illustration below the poem is by Troye
Platt.

26. "My Solemn Vow"—Current statistics indicate that one of
every eight American women will be diagnosed with breast
cancer. Mary was so diagnosed in 1998. In retrospect, Mary
says it was "a gift." This poem, as well as this book, is
dedicated to her with love and admiration.

Index of Titles